Travel Guide

MW01681481

QINGDAO

⊙ Susan Liang William Zou

QINGDAO PUBLISHING HOUSE

图书在版编目（CIP）数据

青岛旅游指南＝Qingdao：英文／梁红等编著.
青岛：青岛出版社，2007.8
ISBN 978-7-5436-4081-8

Ⅰ.青… Ⅱ.①梁… ②邹… Ⅲ.旅游指南－青岛市－英文 Ⅳ.
K928.952.3

中国版本图书馆CIP数据核字（2007）第019029号

It is advisable to keep an eye on the latest information released on the very day when you are traveling in Qingdao since the information provided in this book is apt to change. If you notice any change regarding what is offered in the book, please share with us the updates. Given the fact that effort was taken to make this guide up-to-date at the time of going to print, the Publisher takes no responsibility or liability for any loss, injury or inconvenience incurred by using this guide.

All rights reserved. No part of this publication may be reproduced, stored in a retrieval system or transmitted, in any form or by any means, electronic, mechanical, photocopying, recording or otherwise, without the prior written permission of the publishers and copyright holders.

书　　名　Qingdao
编 著 者　Susan Liang (梁红)　William Zou (邹卫宁)
图片提供　王超鲁　杨文祥　薛晨钟　盛晓平　等
出版发行　青岛出版社
社　　址　青岛市徐州路77号（266071）
本社网址　http://www.qdpub.com
邮购电话　13335059110　(0532)85814611-8664　传真(0532)85814750
责任编辑　杨　慧　E-mail: yh@qdpub.com
装帧设计　杨晓伟
平面制作　杰人平面设计
印　　刷　青岛海尔丰彩印刷有限公司
出版日期　2007年8月第1版　2007年8月第1次印刷
开　　本　1／32（787mm×1092mm）
印　　张　3.75
书　　号　ISBN 978-7-5436-4081-8
定　　价　26.00元

编校质量、盗版监督电话：0532-80998671
青岛版图书售后如发现质量问题，请寄回青岛出版社印刷处调换。
电话：0532-80998826

CONTENTS

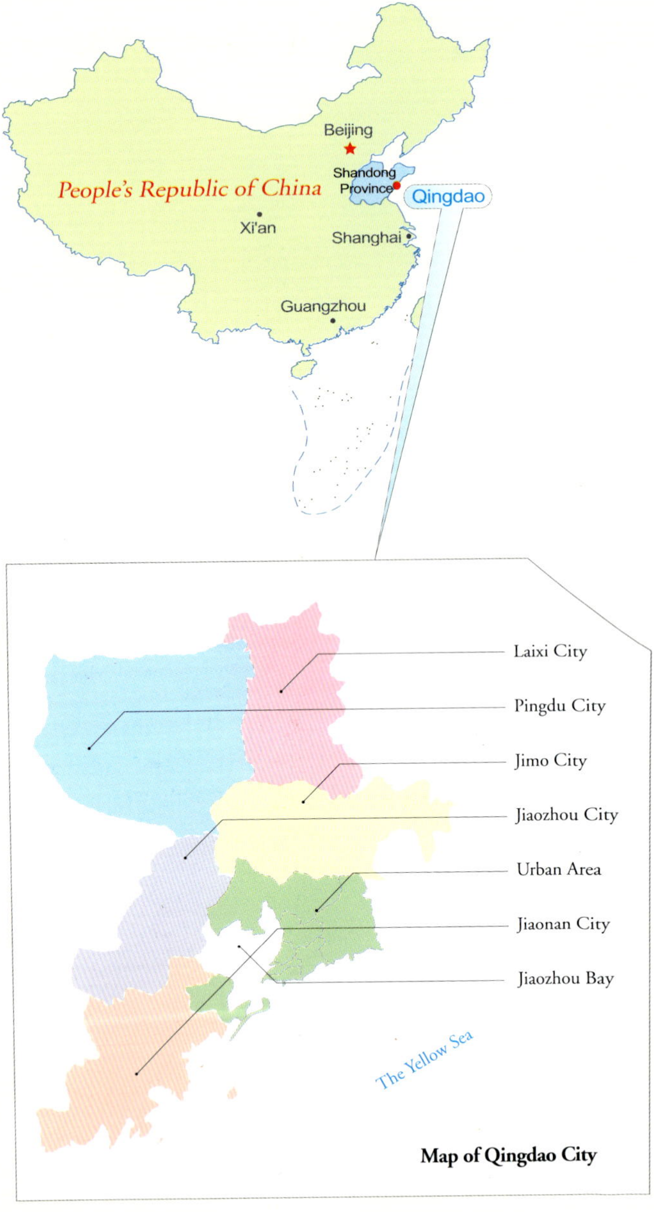

Map of Qingdao City

I. Overview of Qingdao

True to its name, Qingdao, the green island as its name literally suggests, is covered by abundant trees – black pines, chinars, gingkos amid the azure sky and sea.

With green and blue as the natural backdrop, red color stands out as the human creation enhancing the charm of Qingdao, as seen from the red-roofed architecture of various European styles erected during the early 20th Century.

With its soaring architectural triumphs, from the glorious Catholic Church to the magnificent Former German Governor's Residence and the avant-garde spectacle of the 2008 Olympic stadium for the sailing regatta, Qingdao is unique.

Dramas, melodramas, great tragedies and comedies have all been enacted here, on and off the stage. The city played a key role in igniting the May 4th Movement – a national patriotic campaign following the failure of Chinese diplomacy in taking back Qingdao from Germany at the Paris Peace Conference in 1919. The unrivaled scenery of Qingdao serves as a magnet that has drawn and nurtured a number of world-renowned celebrities in arts and literature. Every age has left a legacy of splendid monuments in

Qingdao is located at the mid-south of Shandong Peninsula by the Yellow Sea. It is at 119° 30'E -121° 00'E and 35° 35'N - 37° 09'N. The hilly landscape makes it a charming city between the mountains and the sea. Sea is the major attraction for the holiday-makers, with its close vicinity to the city proper.

Qingdao's Honors

- ★ *Host City for the 29th Olympic Sailing Regatta in 2008*
- ★ *One of the First National Culturally Advanced Cities*
- ★ *Capital of Famous Chinese Brands*
- ★ *China Award for Habitable Environment*
- ★ *A National Model City for Environmental Protection*
- ★ *A National Famous Historical and Cultural City*
- ★ *A National Hygienic City*
- ★ *A National Garden City*
- ★ *One of China's Best Tourist Cities*
- ★ *One of China's Most Popular Cities*
- ★ *China's Most Charming City*

the form of gracious temples and churches.

Qingdao, more than any other city in China, has a centuries-old, ongoing love affair with beautiful and innovative architecture. Yet the real charm of Qingdao comes not only from these magnificent creations, but from the shuttered, balconied boulevards, the winding backstreets, the seaside promenade and the avenues of luxuriant trees.

Qingdao is a city to be savored slowly. Put on comfortable shoes and decide on a certain area before you start out. Allow yourself time to enjoy a century-old florist shop, a corner drugstore, or a delicately carved stone doorway, characterized by the statuesque sketching on the time-honored buildings.

Afraid of getting lost? You will never be far from a bus stop if your feet fail you in the zig-zagging and hilly streets. Sorry to miss one or two sights? It doesn't really matter — they will still be there the next time!

Qingdao, Sailing City

As one of the co-host cities of the 29th Olympic Games, Qingdao, about 800km away from Beijing, will host the sailing event in 2008. In August 2006, Qingdao hosted its first test event for the 29th Olympic Sailing Regatta, the Good Luck Beijing — Qingdao

Below: Sail with heart
Opposite: Recess at sunset

International Regatta (August 18-31) at its Olympic Sailing Center.

One of the most significant decisions in the modern life of Qingdao was made in April 1999 to seek the right to host the 29th Olympic Sailing Regatta as part of Beijing's bid for the 2008 Olympic Games.

Qingdao's residents jubilantly celebrated with Beijing and the whole nation on July 13, 2001, when Beijing was awarded the right to host the 2008 Olympic Games and Paralympic Games. One of the best sailing events in the world will be held in Qingdao with each milestone covered in its preparations for the Games. Five major constructions — the Media Center, the Olympic Athletes' Center, the Olympic Village as well as the Administrative Building and Logistics Center are in place at the 45-hectare Qingdao Olympic Sailing Center on Fushan Bay, the venue of the 29th Olympic Sailing Regatta.

The Media Center and Olympic Athletes' Center were used during the Good Luck Beijing — Qingdao International Regatta 2006. The regatta, involving 300 sail boats and 465 athletes, is a major international Olympic regatta and a test event for the 2008 Olympics in Qingdao. Organized by the Chinese Yachting Association and the Qingdao Municipal Government, it followed the Olympic guidelines of ISAF (the International Sailing Federation) and the Qingdao Race Committee by setting the sailing courses in line with the 2008 Olympic regatta.

Land

It is the work of both nature and man that have given Qingdao its unique charm. The distinctive landscape of mountains against sea has inspired generations of artists who have contributed to the enlightened age of religion and culture. Dongyi People, one of the ancient Chinese tribes, chose to settle here five to six thousand years ago, as the local land and sea gave them good supply of food. This area is a natural trading crossroad and was easily defended in a landscape dominated by numerous hilltops. It is still well situated for travel and transport throughout North China.

The Yellow Sea is the major attraction for holiday-makers, with its close vicinity to the city proper.

Central Qingdao, defined by red roofs, historical constructions and the newly-built seaside promenade, covers a comparatively small area of about 1,102km², one tenth of Greater Qingdao, and has a population of approximately 2.65 million. Central Qingdao lies at the southern coast of the city, a rectangular area stretching from east to west that was the original domain of the German colonists in the early 20th Century.

Below: City of mountains and sea

Today, Greater Qingdao, covering more than 10,654km²,

is made up of Qingdao city proper and five satellite cities: Jimo, Jiaozhou, Jiaonan, Pingdu and Laixi. Greater Qingdao contains about 7.3 million inhabitants, virtually one tenth of the population of Shandong Province. Indeed, Qingdao is one of the most densely populated cities in China.

Hilltops

Nowhere could the landscape of Qingdao be better enjoyed than on the tops of the hills that dot the city proper here and there, including Xinhaoshan (Signal) Hill, Xiaoyushan (Small Fish) Hill, Qingdaoshan Hill, Guanxiangshan (Observatory) Hill and Guanhaishan (Sea-viewing) Hill. At a height of 100-200 meters, these hilltops offer unrivaled viewpoints for the panorama of central Qingdao on a clear day. The national datum mark for altitude measurement is located on the Observatory Hill.

Unlike in other Chinese cities, few bicycle riders are found in the hilly downtown area of Qingdao, where zig-zagging streets run up and down hilly terrain. In addition to 10,000 taxis in service every day, bus travel is also convenient. One yuan is charged for non-airconditioned buses and two yuan for the air-conditioned ones, with dual pricing varying as the seasons alternate.

Local vehicle drivers are used to the ups and downs as well as U-turns

and sharp turns that might otherwise daunt non-native drivers, as these road signs pop up at the end of winding streets, apparently leading them nowhere. Single-way traffic is also typical of Qingdao, where narrow lanes dominate the old city proper. However, preferential treatment is given to taxi drivers who are free to cruise through most of these streets.

Laoshan Mountain

The highest mountain on the coastline of China's Mainland, Laoshan Mountain stands at the southeastern corner of Qingdao, with its peak towering 1,133 meters. Granite boulders are typical of Laoshan, taking on various postures and shapes that resemble and recount a number of scenes and folklores, all of which add to the excellent nature of the mountains. As the cradle of Taoism, Laoshan Mountain is said to be endowed with supernatural talents, as described by Pu Songling (1640-1715), a writer in the Qing Dynasty (1644-1911), in his stories set in Laoshan that have won universal praise.

Sea

Under the umbrella of Laoshan Mountain, the coastline meanders for 730km, comprising capes and bays, of which Jiaozhou Bay is the largest. Stretching 32.5km from north to south and 28 km from east to west, it has an area of $436km^2$.

The Yellow Sea, to the south of Qingdao, is home to the aquiculture of prawn, yellow croaker, hairtail, pomfret and Spanish mackerel, along with such shellfish as clam, mussel, abalone and scallop. A number of local restaurants offer seafood fresh from the sea.

Climate

Influenced by the ocean, the continental monsoon climate takes on a unique look in Qingdao, which has an annual precipitation of 775mm, 80-day cool summer and 149-day mild winter, on average. Along with adequate sunshine, spring and summer are marked with heavy fog, while winter is subject to strong winds. The average temperature in summer is approximately 23℃. The annual number of freezing days is no more than 9.2 on average, from mid-December to early February; mostly caused by cold currents from Siberia.

Opposite: A bird's-eye view of Qingdao
Above: Inviting seafood

As a major seafood distribution center in North China, Qingdao's fishery production tops the country with 300 fishery processors exporting 12 percent of the nationwide total.

Resources

An agreeable climate contributes to the abundant supply of farm produce and mineral resources in Qingdao. Agricultural products include wheat, corn and peanuts. Peanut export ranks first in Shandong Province. Fruit cultivation includes apple, pear, peach apricot, grape, hawthorn and cherry. Grapes grown in Dazeshan Mountain are considered as competitive as those of Turpan in Xinjiang.

Mineral resources range from gold, graphite, and marble to fluorite, zeolite and perlite. The granite particular to Laoshan Mountain was used in such landmark buildings as the Monument to the People's Heroes and the Chairman Mao Memorial Hall in Beijing.

Above: The southern end of Zhongshan Road in the 1920s
Below: Qingdao Village in the late 19th Century
Opposite top-down: Neolithic pitcher with three legs, unearthed in Sanlihe, Jiaozhou City
Copper cooking-ware of the West Zhou Dynasty (1066BC –771BC) unearthed in Jiaonan City
Classroom in the late 19th Century

The mineral water of Laoshan Mountain, noted for its fine quality, is used as the raw material for Tsingtao Beer.

With religious and cultural significance, Qingdao has long been cherished by numerous Taoist followers and artists who have drawn inspiration from the attractive nature here. With Qingdao set as the backdrop, a number of movies and TV plays have been shot here, boosting the city's image.

History

Dongyi People, one of the ancient Chinese tribes, settled in the Qingdao area around five to six thousand years ago, as evidenced by the eggshell basalt unearthed

in Sanlihe, Jiaozhou city. Qi State ruled the area during the Warring States Period (403BC-221BC) before it was united in 221 BC by Emperor Qinshihuang, the first Emperor in China.

The history of the hinterland in Qingdao dates back 5,000 years, although the metropolis itself is only one century old. The May 4th Movement in 1919 staged by the college students in Beijing contributed to the resumption of Qingdao's sovereignty from Germany.

Seafaring was not developed in Qingdao until the Song Dynasty (960–1279) when Qingdao was the only trade seaport in North China, ranking one of the five major ports across the country. Military forces were deployed here as early as the Ming Dynasty (1368–1644) and reinforced in the Qing Dynasty. The year 1891 marked the beginning of the City, when it grew into a key coastal fortress and trade port.

The assassination of two German clergymen by local people in Juye, Shandong Province in 1897, triggered the landing of German troops in Qingdao in the same year, followed by the signing of the *Kiao'ao Concession Treaty* four months later. German Emperor Wilhelm II took the control of the city proper "Tsingtao" in 1898 and opened it to the world as a free trade port. The city was under German administration until 1914, when the Japanese took it by force and continued colonization for eight straight years.

The sovereignty of Qingdao was not regained until 1922, but again fell into Japanese control in 1938.

Backed by the United States, the then Nationalist Government of China assumed direct administration of Qingdao after the surrender of Japan in 1945, turning it into an American military base until 1949, when the People's Republic of China was founded.

Tsingtao Beer

Double - Star

Cultural Relics and Historical Sites

Cultural relics under state protection include the Stele in Tianzhushan (Heaven Pillar) Mountain, the ancient town of Jimo, the Great Wall of the ancient Qi State (403BC–221BC), the Badaguan Scenic Spot, and the Former Residence & Administration Headquarters of the German Governor.

A number of sites are under protection of the state, province and municipality, of which some are open to the public, such as the Stele at Tianzhushan Mountain, Sanlihe and Langyatai. Modern sites are located mainly in the downtown area, such as Xiaoqingdao Lighthouse, Kang Youwei Tomb, the German Emplacement, the Observatory and the Water Datum Mark.

Economy

Fortune rated Qingdao the seventh among China's best business cities, saying that with its irreproducible geographic location and beautiful environment, Qingdao has the cutting edge in administrative efficiency, business cost and urban infrastructure — a city that promises well.

As a foreign trade port and a national marine science center, Qingdao is one of the 14 coastal cities opened up to the world and one of the eight international conference centers nationwide. The local economies of port logistics and tourism are gaining momentum alongside the major industries of electrical appliances, petrochemical, automobiles, shipbuilding, telecommunications, food and drinks.

Qingdao is China's largest manufacturing base for household appliances. The Oil Refinery boasts China's

Qingdao is a city where one can be flooded with famous brands any time. The brands created here have influence across China and are making thier way into the outside world.
Qingdao has been rated by CCTV as one of China's Top Ten Economically Dynamic Cities and won the Award for Entrepreneur Satisfaction.

first 10-million-tonne project in the 21st Century. The Haixiwan Shipbuilding Project, with 7.4 billion yuan (nearly one billion US dollars) investment, has an annual production capacity of 4.7 million deadweight tonnes. A total of 500 million US dollars has been invested in the International Container Wharf at Qianwan Port in Huangdao District.

Above: Sand sculpture
Opposite: Top famous brands of Qingdao

Tsingtao Beer and Haier (white goods manufacturer) are among the most renowned brands in China and the world, in addition to Double-star (footwear), Hisense (electrical appliances), Etsong (tobacco) and Aucma (freezers). Beer of various tastes is offered at the Tsingtao Brewery Museum, and a visit to the Haier Museum will acquaint you with its modern management and corporate culture.

People

Qingdao remained no more than a small fishing village for thousands of years until a century ago when it began to prosper in economy that gave rise to the increase of population.

The immigrant inflow drawn by the beautiful environment bears relation to the numerous talents particularly in the circles of art and athletics.

The history of immigration can be traced back to the Qin Dynasty some 2,000 years ago. Immigration to Qingdao boomed in the Ming Dynasty with most of the immigrants arriving from Yunnan province in Southwest China, as a result of manpower demand to cement coastal defense that contributed to the trade

prosperity of Qingdao at that time.

Two major immigration booms occurred in 1891-1922 and 1922-1937. Population in the former period reached 170,000 with the inflow of craftsmen from South China, while the latter period was dominated by immigrants from within the province. There were already 700,000 inhabitants in Qingdao by 1949 when the People's Republic of China was founded.

Tall, good-looking and well-built, the local people are talented in athletics, in particular, track and field events. Qingdao is considered a football city and water sport center. The artistic atmosphere has brought up a number of artists such as Lu Siqing, the world famous violinist.

Above: Spring Festival pictures of Pingdu City
Below: Hollowed out gourd

Overseas Exchange

Viewed historically as an international city, Qingdao was home to the consulates of a dozen countries in the

City	Country	Date of Establishment	City	Country	Date of Establishment
Shimonoseki	Japan	Oct. 3, 1979	Puerto Montt	Chile	Aug. 17, 1999
Long Beach	USA	Apr. 12, 1985	Montevideo	Uruguay	Apr. 15, 2004
Acapulco	Mexico	Aug. 21, 1985	Klaipeda	Lithuania	Apr. 15, 2004
Odessa	Ukraine	Apr. 29, 1993	Bilbao	Spain	Aug. 21, 2004
Daegu	R.O.K	Dec. 4, 1993	Nantes	France	Jun. 4, 2005
Ness-Ziona	Israel	Dec. 2, 1997	Miami	USA	Aug. 30, 2005
Velsen	Netherlands	Dec. 9, 1998	Brest	France	May 8, 2006
Southampton	UK	Dec. 27, 1998			

early 20th Century. At present, it houses the Consulate General of ROK and has developed 15 sister cities of 13 countries including Shimonoseki, Japan and Long Beach, USA.

Folk Customs

Qingdao's local culture features innovation and compatibility thanks to its situation at the forefront of opening up to the outside world, and its immigration history of blending with foreign cultures. Some terms that were borrowed from German are still in use today, when the elderly locals chat with each other in Qingdao dialect such as "*guli*" derived from the German word "gully", meaning "drainage".

Qingdao boasts a unique catering style of beer-drinking together with seafood. Enjoying more fame abroad than the city itself, Tsingtao Beer — a century-old brand established with a German recipe and technology — remains one of the leading industries and consumer commodities in the city. It is a common practice that, at the commencement of a dinner, the host proposes three toasts to the guests at the table as the lead-in of the dinner and all the participants are expected to drink together in response.

The influence of foreign culture is expressed nowhere better than in architecture. Qingdao is seen as an expo of architecture left by its colonial history. It is said that styles of 24 countries are available at Badaguan alone while the local courtyard style — the three-storey buildings at each of the

four sides — is typical of the mid-town area. The newly developed area refers to the eastern part of the city ruled by skyscrapers.

The sea nourishes all creature, as seen from a common scene in winter when people and birds co-exist harmoniously on the beach of Qingdao. The public campaign of feeding seagulls at Zhanqiao Pier has attracted more seafowl to stay here for the winter.

The local folk art involves paper cut and operas, as well as Jiaozhou Gong and Drum, and Yangge — folk dances popular in the suburban areas. Like the Christmas carol in western countries, Taoist believers composed their own sacred music at Laoshan Mountain in ancient times, which has been staged since its restoration.

Historical and Contemporary Figures

The beautiful environment attracts a number of statesmen — the First Emperor of China and Emperor Wudi of the Han Dynasty (206BC–220AD), as well as men of letters such as Li Bai of the Tang Dynasty (618–907), Su Shi of the Song Dynasty and Gu Yanwu of the Ming Dynasty. Pu Songling of the Qing Dynasty created *Liao Zhai Zhi Yi*, a collection of ghost stories, some of which are set at Taiqing Palace of Laoshan Mountain. Gao Fenghan, one of the *Eight Eccentrics of Yangzhou*, was from Sanlihe, Jiaozhou City, where a memorial honors his feat in the quadruplet of *qin-chess-calligraphy-painting*.

Richard Wilhelm (1873-1930), German Sinologist, opened the spiritual secrets of China to the West through his translations of the *I Ching* and the Taoist works of *The Secret of the Golden Flower* during his stay in Qingdao. His legacy of Chinese philosophy has passed on and he is valued for his contribution to the education in Qingdao in the early 20th Century.

Kang Youwei, calligrapher and reformist in the late Qing Dynasty spent his later years in Qingdao, after he retreated from the imperial court.

The 1930s saw the boom of the local economy and culture, seen from a swarm of the writers and educators here such as Wen Yiduo, Lao She, Shen Congwen, Xiao Jun, Xiao Hong, Liang Shiqiu, as well as some renowned scientists in physics, biology and astronomy. Visiting the Former Residences of the Men of Letters in downtown Qingdao revives the once-brilliant life of the men of letters during the 1930s.

Modern Qingdao is noted for its marine science research marked by 24 academicians of Chinese Academy of Sciences and Chinese Academy of Engineering.

Zhang Ruimin, CEO of Haier Group, is the name card of Qingdao.

Opposite: Kang Youwei (1858–1927), calligrapher and reformist, stayed at Qingdao in the 1920s
Below:
The Zhougezhuang Sail-setting Festival

The Candied Hawthorn Fair at Haiyun Nunnery is the most celebrated local festivity after the Spring Festival.
The Zhougezhuang Sail-setting Festival ranks the most spectacular one of its kind in Shandong Peninsula

Local Festivities

Most festivities originated from the religious temple fairs, of which the **Candied Haw Fair** at Haiyun'an Nunnery stands out. On the sixteenth of the Lunar January, it features the trade of strings of sugar-coated haws. The Fair once entered into the Top 100 Tourist Attractions of the China Tourism Administration.

Dazeshan Stone Festival Pingdu City, March 16th, Lunar Year

Shimei'an Plum Blossom Festival, Licang District, mid-March

Zhougezhuang Sail-setting Festival Jimo City, March 18, Lunar Calendar

Cherry Blossom Festival Zhongshan Park, late April to early May

International Kite-flying Contest Golden Beach of Huangdao District, April

Above: Radish sculpture at Radish Festival
Below: Qingdao International Maritime Expo

Laoshan Mountain Tourism and Culture Festival Exhibitions and fairs of tea, cherry, fruit blossoms, as well as mountain-climbing activities, April 25 — June 10

Zhanshansi Temple Fair Buddhist Festival, April 8th, Lunar Calendar

China Electronics Show A Sino-US joint event, International Conventional Center, July

Qingdao Marine Festival Exhibitions and forums on marine culture, water sports, marine tourism, sea food cuisine as well as aquaculture, July

Qingdao Summer Art Festival Art performances, July, Shinan District

Qingdao International Beer Festival Beer-drinking and merry-making activities, late August to early September

Qingdao International Sand Sculpture Festival No.1 Bathing Beach, September

II. Beach and City

Qingdao has long been crowned the Pearl of the Yellow Sea and the Swiss in the East, which is self-evident with the unfolding of the panorama that features mountains, seas, European-styled city and the suburbs with rich cultural heritage. The scenic spots are centralized along the coastline of Qingdao and the Laoshan Mountain.

As the host city for the sailing regatta of the 29th Olympics in 2008, Qingdao has developed fine water sports training facilities – an ideal venue for waterborne competitions. A sailboat or a sailboard is always available on the beach if one wants to experience the excitement of sailing in the sea.

Special Excursions

Taking a cruise provides access to some islands, where the natural beauty is enchanting. A small number of islands (among the total of 50) have been developed for tourism, offering activities like fishing and island exploration.

Water Sports The beaches of Qingdao are home to such waterborne events as swimming, sailing, surfing and yachting.

Sanatoriums The agreeable climate in Qingdao is unrivaled for rehabilitation.

Fishing at Sea The bays and islands offer good prospects for rodsters, especially in autumn. Try your luck in the fishing competition – you might end up winning the top prize!

Religion As the birthplace of the Quanzhen Sect of Taoism, Laoshan Mountain helps you experience the Tao's essentiality. It was here that Taoism really took root, and many ancient temples and monasteries were constructed here. Other religious sites are Zhanshan Temple and Fahai Temple. Western religions were also established at the beginning of the last century, in such shrines as Catholic Church and Christian Church, together with a mosque downtown near Dongfang Hotel.

Education and Research Qingdao has a dozen institutions on marine scientific research, boasting 40% of the marine professionals across the country. About 1/3 marine institutes in China are based in Qingdao such as Ocean University of China and Institute of Oceanology under Chinese Academy of Sciences. Sinology is offered in OUC and Qingdao University for overseas students who may also work toward masters or Ph.D degrees in marine-related disciplines.

Architecture Some buildings in downtown Qingdao erected during the German Occupation 100 years ago boast the European architectural

styles of over 20 countries such as the Former German Governor's Residence, the Headquarters of German Administration (the present NPC and CPPCC Qingdao Committee), the Christian Church and the Catholic Church (St. Michael's Cathedral). The former site of Red Swastika (Qingdao), now the Qingdao Art Gallery, is a masterpiece, combining three styles of Chinese, Roman and Arabic.

Noted recently as a wedding backdrop, Badaguan is bustling all year round, May Day in particular. On fine and warm days, it is alive with wedding couples being photographed and videoed.

The old city proper along the seashore and Badaguan Villa Area are dominated by the foreign-styled constructions that are easy of access.

Romantic Honeymoon at Seaside It is a paradise for newly-weds to enjoy their honeymoon.

Top-down: Wind of May Xiaoqingdao Zhanqiao Pier Opposite: Entertainment on the beach

Top Ten Downtown Scenic Spots

Wind of May The May 4th Square by the Fushan Bay is marked by the huge flaming sculpture called Wind of May.

Badaguan Villa Area A number of western historical buildings characterize this area of luxuriant trees, with the eight roads named after eight historically well-known passes in China.

Xiaoqingdao (Small Qingdao Island) Verdant trees and grass cover this tiny island, which is highlighted by a white lighthouse – an engaging view at night.

Huilange (Wave-rippling Pavilion) of Zhanqiao Pier Extending 400 meters into the sea, the Pier ends with a two-storey pavilion, the symbol of Qingdao.

No.1 Bathing Beach Accommodating tens of thousands of swimmers, the Beach is a spectacular scene in the summer, enhanced by the picturesque backdrop of Lu Xun Park.

Seaside Sculpture Museum The exotic display of sculptures at the seaside takes on a splendor against the golden color of the setting sun.

TV Tower Topping Taiping (Peace) Hill, the steel Tower dominates the downtown area as an inspiration for tourists.

Lanchaoge Pavilion Towering above Xiaoyushan (Small Fish) Hill by the sea, the Pavilion claims the best view of the bright moon rising above the sea, with the twin moons reflecting each other between water and sky—a view best presented on the Chinese Mid-autumn Festival.

Century Square Linked one after another, the squares look like a string of pearls shining on the newly-developed eastern area.

Xinhaoshan Hill The resplendent panorama of sunset glow on the city can only be obtained on the Hill where the Former German Governor's Residence and the three torch-like watch towers are gilded in the sunset rays—best illustrated in February to August of the Chinese lunar calendar.

Proposed Itineraries in the Downtown Area

One-day Tour

Route A: Zhongyuan Square, Zhanqiao Pier, a cruise along the coast, Xiaoqingdao Park, Navy Museum, Underwater World, Marine Products Museum, Xiaoyushan Park, Badaguan Villa Area, May 4th Square, Music Square, seaside sculptures along Donghai Road, Qingdao Museum

Route B: Zhongyuan Square, Zhanqiao Pier, Catholic Church, Navy Museum, Underwater World, Xiaoyushan Park, May 4th Square, seaside sculptures along Donghai Road, Polar Ocean World

Route C: Zhongyuan Square, Zhanqiao Pier, Tianhougong (the Marine Goddess) Palace, Christian Church, Former Residence of the German Governor, Former Site of German Emplacement on Qingdao Hill, Zhongshan Park, TV Tower, Zhanshan Temple, May 4th Square, Polar Ocean World

Riding buses is convenient for a sightseeing tour in the downtown area, along with taking a taxi. Since most of the scenic spots are scattered along the seaside, it is advisable to take a walk along the Seaside Promenade from Badaxia (named after the eight gorges) and Zhanqiao Pier, to the May 4th Square, where all the downtown scenic spots are contained.

Below: European-styled old city proper

Route D: Zhongyuan Square, Zhanqiao Pier, Badaguan Villa Area, seaside sculptures along Donghai Road, May 4th Square, Polar Ocean World, Qingdao Museum

Two-day Tour

Route A:

Day 1: Zhongyuan Square, Zhanqiao Pier, a cruise off the coast, Xiaoqingdao Park, Navy Museum, Underwater World, Marine Products Museum, Xiaoyushan Park, Zhongshan Park, Badaguan Villa Area, No.1 Bathing Beach

Day 2: Christian Church, Former Residence of the German Governor, Former Residence of Kang Youwei, Former Site of German Emplacement on Qingdao Hill, seaside sculptures along Donghai Road, May 4th Square, Polar Ocean World

Route B:

Day 1: Zhongyuan Square, Zhanqiao Pier, Catholic Church, Former Residence of the German Governor, Christian Church, Xinhaoshan Park, Former Site of German Emplacement on Qingdao Hill, Navy Museum, Marine Products Museum

Day 2: Badaguan Villa Area, seaside sculptures along Donghai Road, May 4th Square, Music Square, Polar Ocean World, Shilaoren (the Old Stone Man) Beach, Qingdao Museum

Opposite: Red-roofed residences amid green trees
Above: Group sculptures at Langyatai

Three-day Tour

Route A:

Day 1: Zhanqiao Pier, a cruise off the coast, Xiaoqingdao Park, the Navy Museum, Underwater World, Marine Products Museum, Badaguan Villa Area, No.1 Bathing Beach

Day 2: Catholic Church, Former Site of the Headquarters of the German Administration, Christian Church, Former Residence of the German Governor, Tianhougong Palace, Former Site of German Emplacement on Qingdao Hill, Xiaoyushan Park, Zhongshan Park, TV Tower, Zhanshan Temple, National Forest Park

Day 3: Seaside sculptures along Donghai Road, May 4th Square, Polar Ocean World, Qingdao Museum

Route B:

Day 1: Zhanqiao Pier, Catholic Church, Former Site of the Headquarters of the German Administration, Christian Church, Former Residence of the German Governor, Tianhougong Palace, Former Site of German Emplacement on Qingdao Hill, Badaguan Villa Area, No.1 Bathing Beach

Day 2: A cruise off the coast, Navy Museum, Underwater World, Marine Products Museum, Luxun Park, Xiaoyushan Park, Former Residence of Kang Youwei, Former Residence of Wen Yiduo

Day 3: Seaside sculptures along Donghai Road, May 4th Square, Polar Ocean World, Qingdao Museum

Scenic Spots along the Seaside

Seaside Promenade

A newly-built plank promenade meanders along the southern beach for about 40 km, from Tuandao Cape in southwestern Qingdao to Shilaoren Holiday Resort in the eastern part of the city. Defining the geography, architecture and whole fibre of Qingdao, the Promenade wanders slowly through the best scenes of Qingdao, languidly accepting all tributes.

Now let's start our tour from the western part of the city, covering Qingdao Bay, Huiquan Bay, Taiping Bay and comes to an end at the Newly-developed eastern

area.

Scenic Spots along Qingdao Bay

Zhanqiao Pier Built as a wharf in the late 19th century, the 440-meter pier takes on the distinctive Chinese style with an octagonal Huilange (Wave-rippling) Pavilion added to its end in the 1930s, a symbol of Qingdao.

Former Site of the Headquarters of the German Administration Constructed during 1903-1906 under the design of a German architect, it is of the 19th Century European style of public utilities. This site was the office building of the Qingdao Municipal People's Government from 1949 (when the People's Republic of China was founded) to 1994, when it became the office of the NPC and CPPCC Qingdao Committee. It has been under the protection of the State Administration for the Preservation of Cultural and Historical Relics since 1996.

Former Residence of the German Governor Following the German castle design of European royal style, the building was under construction from 1903-1908. It was used as the residence of the German governor in Kiaochow (Jiaozhou Bay). Situated at the tableland south of Xinhaoshan Hill,

Opposite above:Seaside Promenade
Opprosite below:Sketch map of Qingdao Bay
Above:Former Site of the Headquarters of the German Administration
Below: Former Residence of the German Governor

it is of an asymmetrical plane, on which light yellow external walls of concrete are strikingly dominated by huge pieces of granite, while the interior decoration is of European style. It was opened to the public in May, 1999.

Tianhougong (The Marine Goddess) Palace Built on the present Taiping Road in 1467, it houses a museum for folk art exhibition and a shrine where the traditional Marine Goddess was worshipped for the safe return of the fishing boats in the ancient times. As one of the oldest constructions existing in Qingdao, this palace is under the municipal-level protection of cultural and historical relics since 1982.

Below: Tianhougong Palace
Opposite top-down: Christian Church Catholic Church Former Site of Red Swastika(Qingdao)

Former Site of Red Swastika (Qingdao) Located at 37 Yushan Road, this site used to be Qingdao Museum before it turns into Qingdao Gallery. Featuring unique architectural design, its three courtyards are respectively of the Roman, traditional Chinese, and Arabic styles.

Xiaoqingdao (Small Qingdao Island) Park Southeast of Zhanqiao Pier, covering an area of 0.012km^2, this park has become another symbol of Qingdao, alongside the Pier. Shaped like a heptachord, it is also dubbed "Heptachord Island".

Navy Museum The 40,000m^2 Museum at 8 Laiyang Road houses the largest navy-related collections in China, including uniforms, weapons, and submarines, as well as missiles. The museum showcases the history and development of the Chinese People's Navy.

Cruise Wharf on Laiyang Road Tour yachts are offered here for the tourists to have an overview of the Qingdao Bay and Taiping Bay while cruising among Xiaoqingdao, Lu Xun Park and Taiping Cape along the coast.

People's Hall Modeled after the Great Hall of the People in Beijing, People's Hall functions as a theater on Taiping Road.

Catholic Church Built on Zhejiang Road in the 1930s, it has two bell towers, one on each side of the church. The church, including the huge cross situated on top, rises to a height of 60 meters. Religious activities take place on regular basis.

Christian Church Completed in 1910 for religious services for the Germans, Christian Church is otherwise called the German Auditorium. It comprises the bell tower and the church hall. The 39-meter-high bell tower has a huge clock on each of its three sides. The two-storey main body of the church hall is 18 meters high.

Guanxiangshan (Observatory) Hill This hill is named after the Observatory built on top of it by the Germans in 1905. Amid the

Enjoying the scenery on the downtown hills is particular to Qingdao tourism, where tourists can overlook scenic spots that they plan to visit, or have just visited. Looking afar on the top of Xinhaoshan, one can appreciate the beauty of the undulating mountain ranges and red roofs, as well as the green trees of the old city proper, highlighted by the glow of the sunset.

beautiful environment, it is a base for research and education of astronomy and meteorology. It is under the administration of Nanjing Zijinshan (Purple Mountain) Observatory, CAS.

Xinhaoshan (Signal Hill) Park Following the construction of Qingdao Port, signal banners were hoisted on the Hill for fishermen and ships on the sea. The mushroom-shaped towers claim an unrivaled view of the architecture and scenery in Qingdao. The park is accessible from both Longshan Road and Qidong Road.

Former Residence of Wang Tongzhao Wang created his famous novel *Rain in the Mountain* and many other works during his 30-year stay at 49 Guanhai 2nd Road.

Former Residence of Xiao Hong, Xiao Jun and Shu Qun The Xiaos and the Shus were neighbors at 1 Guanxiang 1st Road during the years 1934-1935, when they produced milestone works in modern Chinese literature.

Former Residence of Lao She Rated the renowned writer of contemporary times, Lao She stayed at 12 Huangxian Road from 1934-1937, writing the novel *Camel Xiangzi*.

Opposite above: Marine Products Museum
Opposite below: The national datum mark for altitude measurement on Guanxiangshan Hill
Below: Sketch map of Huiquan Bay

Guanhaishan (Sea View Hill) Park Accessible from Guanhai 2nd Road, the park serves as a base for marine education, in addition to being a sightseeing spot.

Lao She Park Covering an area of more than 9,600m^2 along Anhui Road, the park is divided by Hubei Road into two sections, each featuring its own view.

Scenic Spots along Huiquan Bay

Marine Products Museum Located inside Lu Xun Park, the Museum consists of a city-gate-like tower and a palace, both of the ancient Chinese style. The Aquarium, built in 1932 and containing five exhibition halls, is the only aquarium in China which specializes in breeding and showcasing marine creatures.

Underwater World Adjacent to Lu Xun Park and No.1 Bathing Beach, Underwater World (formerly known as Marine Products Museum), at 2 Laiyang Road, covers an area of 7,000m^2, and accommodates a waterbody of 4,000 tonnes.

Lu Xun Park Completed in 1929, this is a seaside park built in line with the natural landscape stretching from Xiaoqingdao to No.1 Bathing Beach. The statue of Lu Xun, the most influential Chinese writer

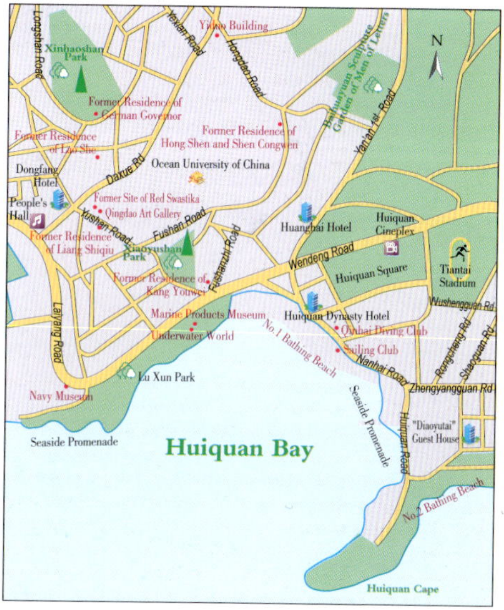

of the early 20th Century, faces the front gate.

Xiaoyushan (Small Fish Hill) Park On the west of Huiquan Bay stands Xiaoyushan Hill, which features frescos depicting legends of fish, as well as an 18-meter-high pavilion.

No.1 Bathing Beach The 3.6-hectare Beach at Huiquan Bay is one of the most famous beaches in Qingdao, with its changing rooms built underground, their roofs forming part of the Seaside Promenade.

Huiquan Square Next to Huiquan Bay is the 45-hectare Square, dubbed the Sitting

Room of the City, thanks to the well-equipped entertainments of body-building, catering and cinema.

The Sailing Club At 6 Nanhai Road, it is perfectly located for gorgeous sunsets, views of No.1 Beach and wind surfers. With a seafood-based English menu, you can dine along the boardwalk or on the terrace — the only way to end a day or start a night on a clear Qingdao afternoon.

Highlights involve prawn & scallops skewers, seafood salad as well as jet ski hire and training for sailing, windsurfing. The best time to hang around is sipping cocktails whilst the sun sets. You can even do "people watch" as the seaside boardwalk passes near by.

The Sailing Club was founded by the Qingdao Marine Sport School under the State Physical Culture Administration. As a major training base for China National Sailing and Surfing Teams and for other sailing clubs all over the world, it is also one of the hosting clubs for various individual Regatta World Championships of the World Sailing Association. Now for those who have never

Xiaoyushan Park commands the finest prospect of Huiquan Bay and the architecture in the city. Across the sea looms Phoenix Island to the south; to the east, a vista of No.1 Bathing Beach and Huiquan Bay. A glance to the north reveals a panorama of red roofs and swaying green trees, with flocks of pigeons flying above – a truly unique scene of elegance and beauty.

Opposite above: Xiaoyushan Park
Opposite below: No.1 Bathing Beach
Below: Huiquan Square

sailed before, the Sailing Club offers lessons as well as the boats to learn from — the Optimist, for example. Prices range from 60-180 RMB/hour depending on the class of boat you choose to rent for the day. There is also a large selection of windsurfing equipment to give the best or the absolute worst windsurfer a chance to make a stud or fool out of themselves for a mere 50 RMB/hour (tack on a lesson for 20 RMB, it's worth it). If the water is too cold, then there are wet suits for renting. The Sailing Club also offers private tours of Qingdao via the coastline, fishing trips, jet skis, and parasailing.

Qinhai Diving Club Located near No. 1 Bathing Beach, Qingdao Qinhai Diving Club provides all kinds of ocean recreation and fishing expeditions and is the only government certified deep-sea diving club in north China. The instructors at Qinhai Diving Club have national level training certificates and use only the best international brands of equipment, all to ensure your safety. The club also has a well-appointed lounge, game room, business conference center and a magnificent seaside deck platform commanding Huiquan Bay. Training is offered for deep-sea diving CMAS certificate.

Opposite above: Ocean University of China
Opposite below: Yiduo Building
Above: Tiantai Stadium
Below: Former Residence of Kang Youwei

Tiantai Stadium Built in the 1930s to the east of Huiquan Square, the Stadium is patterned after the Los Angeles Stadium in the USA. Its capacity of almost 20,000 people ranked it the largest sports venue in Qingdao for a long period of time.

Ocean University of China As one of the key universities in China, with its own features of marine and fishery science, OUC takes pride in its beautiful Yushan campus, designed in accordance with the rise and fall of the landscape. The university has two other campuses in the eastern part of the city.

Yiduo Building Named after Wen Yiduo at the northeastern corner of the OUC campus, it is the former residence of Wen Yiduo, who was a famous scholar of the early 20th Century and once served as Dean of the Humanities College of the then Qingdao University.

Former Residence of Shen Congwen, writer of 1930s A two-storey building at 3 Fushan Road, this building witnessed the creation of Shen's literary works, including the incubation of *The Frontier City* in 1931.

Former Residence of Liang Shiqiu, writer and translator Liang inhabited

33 Yushan Road, from 1930 to 1934, while he worked on *The Literary & Artistic Critic Collection* and the translation of *The Complete Works of William Shakespeare.*

Former Residence of Kang Youwei (1858 – 1927) Kang Youwei, famous scholar and reformist of the Qing Dynasty, stayed at 5 Fushan Zhi Road for some time each year after he bought it in 1923. The house had been the former residence of the Aide to German Governor. It is several minutes' walk from the No.1 Bathing Beach.

Scenic Spots Around Taiping Hill and Badaguan Villa Area

Taiping (Peace) Hill A fairly high hill in Qingdao, Taiping Hill has been developed into what is called One Tower (TV Tower) and Four Parks.

Zhongshan Park Between Huiquan Square and Taiping Hill, it is the largest park downtown, best known for its cherry blossoms in the spring, lantern show in the summer, and chrysanthemum show in the autumn. Two cableways provide the tourists an opportunity to appreciate the view from the air.

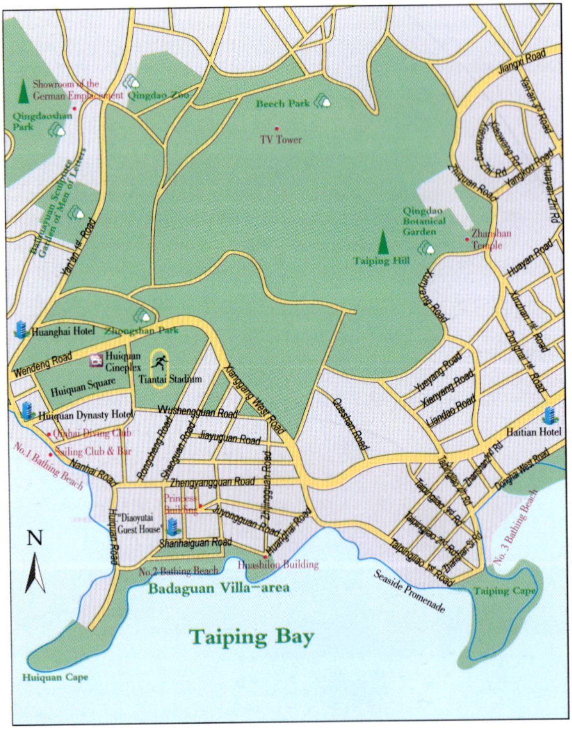

Qingdaoshan (Qingdao Hill) Park Northwest of

Zhongshan Park, the Hill is 128.5 meters high, second to Taiping Hill. Two emplacements built during the German Occupation and an underground military headquarters are open to the public.

Showroom of the German Emplacement on Qingdao Hill In 1977 (centennial of the German invasion) a showroom was built at the foot of Qingdao Hill before it was renovated and restored to what it had been a century ago.

Qingdao Zoo The 300,000m^2 Zoo to the north of Zhongshan Park houses a host of rare and precious animals.

Qingdao Botanical Garden Between Zhongshan Park and Zhanshan Temple, more than a thousand species of plants are raised in an area of 689,310m^2, on which amusement functions for exploration and body-building add to its fascination.

Baihuayuan Sculpture Garden of Men of Letters A newly developed recreation place between Qingdao Hill and Zhongshan Park is dotted with 20 sculptures of men of letters who once inhabited Qingdao, including Pu Songling, Kang Youwei, Wang

Opposite: Sketch map of Taiping Hill and Badaguan Villa Area
Top-down: Former Site of German Emplacement on Qingdao Hill
Zhongshan Park
Zhanshan Temple

Tongzhao, Wen Yiduo, Lao She and Shen Congwen.

Rock Climbing Arena Housed inside the China Marine Sports School at 1 Wuchang Road, the man-made cliff challenges the brave and the strong.

Zhanshan Temple Built in the early 1930s to the east of the Botanical Garden, it is considered the youngest temple of the Tiantai Sect of Chinese Buddhism. It has five courtyards and a seven-storey pagoda. The Temple Fair on April 8th of the Chinese lunar calendar attracts hundreds of thousands of people.

Beech Park North of Taiping (Pacific) Hill, Beech Park is covered with exuberant trees, particularly beech.

TV Tower Ranked the No.1 Iron Tower in China, the 230-meter-high tower is erected at the altitude of 110 meters on Taiping Hill. The rotating watch tower at the 160-meter level offers a bird's-eye view of the city.

Huiquan Cape This cape is presently an ideal place to appreciate the moon amid the lofty pine trees growing on steep rocks. During the German occupation, however, emplacements were deployed at this gateway to Jiaozhou Bay. The East Sea Hotel, built here in the 1930s, boasted the highest and most renowned hotel at that time.

Noted recently as a wedding backdrop, Badaguan is bustling all year round, May Day in particular. On fine and warm days, it is alive with wedding couples being photographed and videoed.

Badaguan Villa Area As a villa area developed in late 1920s east of Huiquan Bay, Badaguan is reputed for its "Architectural Expo" as well as its tranquil and beautiful environment where roads named after eight mountain passes in China are all lined with different trees.

No. 2 Bathing Beach Bordering on the Badaguan Villa Area, it is smaller than the No.1 Bathing Beach, but under a hotter pursuit for ceremony photography during the peak wedding season.

Opposite above: TV Tower
Opposite below: Autumn at Badaguan
Below: Huashilou Building after snow

Huashilou Building Constructed in the 1930s to the east of No.2 Bathing Beach, the five-storey building is of European castle style, decorated with cobblestones on the external wall.

Qingdao "Diaoyutai Guest House" An American style building at 9 Shanhaiguan (Mountain-and-Sea Pass) Road, this guest house has accommodated a number of foreign state leaders and officials, thus named after the State Guest House in Beijing.

Princess Building The building at 16 Juyongguan Road, was designed in the 1930s by the Danish

Consulate in Qingdao for the Danish princess, although she failed to make her presence here.

Taiping (Peace) Cape The architecture and greenery along the ten roads in this area bear remarkable likeness to the Badaguan Villa Area except that the capes and bays here are a favorite haunt of anglers.

No. 3 Bathing Beach Eastward of No. 2 Bathing Beach is another beach ordinally ranked the third, featuring clear water and fine sand.

Newly-developed Area in the Eastern Part of the City

City Hall Completed in 1992, the imposing building cluster won the highest construction award nationwide – Lu Ban Award (named after Lu Ban, a famous carpenter in ancient China).

Yinhai International Yacht Club In accordance with international standards, the marina has 366 normal yacht berths under planning, 130 of which were put into operation in June 2005 by Aister Marine, a Spanish company. The marina offers charging, refueling, fresh water filling, boat servicing and slip way, in addition to a boating school and heli-port. Facilities include restaurants, hotels, Karaoke, cafés, bars, fishing pool, beauty gyms, business centers, sailors' apartments, bathing and health centers, an indoor swimming pool and a yacht training school.

Donghai Road This is a 12.8km seaside road in the eastern part of the city, featuring green areas and 15 sculpture gardens.

May 4th Square Represented by the sculpture Wind of May, the Square opposite the City Hall was named in memory of the May 4th Movement (1919) for regaining the sovereignty of Qingdao.

Xianggang Road From Zhongshan Park on the west to Shilaoren Beach on the east, Xianggang Road is a sightseeing boulevard with a greening area of 200,000m^2.

Music Square A seaside square with an elegant environment, the Square is dedicated to musical activities and performances, facilitated by a fixed giant

Opposite above: Princess Building
Opposite Below: City Hall
Above: Seaside villas along Donghai Road
Below: Sketch map of the eastern part of the city

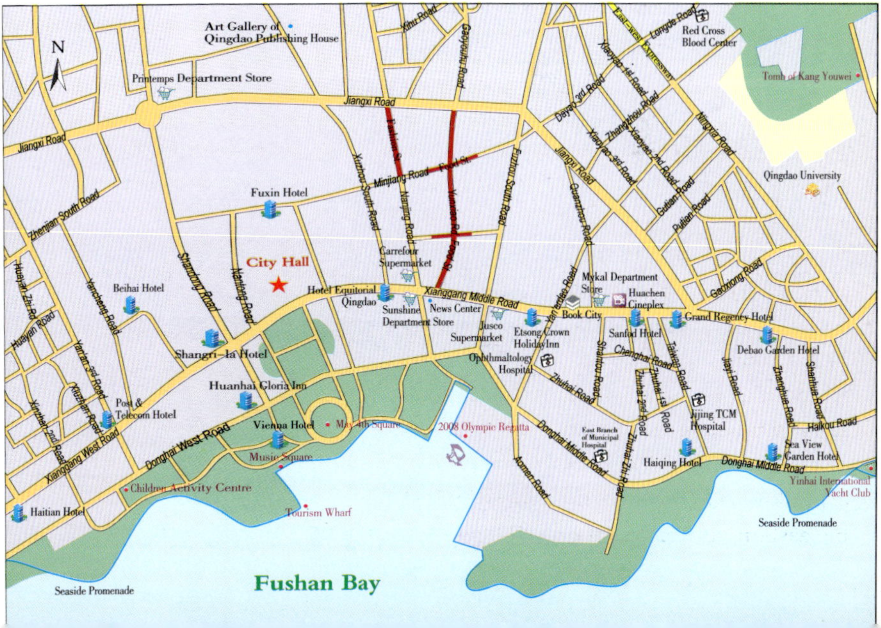

International Golf Cours
Liaoyang West Road
Yinchuan East Road
Xianxialing Road
Qingdao International Convention Center
Time Square
Haier Sci-tech Museum
Municipal Museum
Songling Road
Etsong Stadium
East Station for Long-distance Bus
Yinchuan West Road
Haier Road
Lishan East Road
Miaoling Road
Qinling Road
Meiling Road
Yunling Road
International Beer City
Shilaoren Sight-seeing Park
Fushan Mountain
Shilaoren Bathing Beach
Shilaoren (Old Stone Man) Holiday Resort
Seaside Promenade
Haikou Road
Haining Road
Shilaoren (Old Stone Ma
Hai'an Road
Hailong Road
Qingdao Seaside Sculpture Museum
Haiqing Road
N
Haichuan Road
Haikou Road
Xianggang East Road
Haijiang Road
ina Ocean
iversity
Haikou Road
Seaside Promenade
Donghai East Road
Polar Ocean World
Legend
Main road
Special Street
Seaside Promenade
East-west Highway
Scenic spots
Mountains
City Hall
Airport
Railway station
Long-distance bus station
Ferry
University
Hotel
Hospital
Cinema
Music hall, Theater
Shop & Supermarket
Library, Book shop
Park
Sports center
Olympic Sailing Center

piano and the statue of Nie'er, who composed China's national anthem.

Qingdao University At the southwest foot of Fushan Mountain, the 1,000,000m² University was founded in 1985 and expanded in 1993 by merging with Qingdao Textile Institute, Qingdao Medical Institute and Qingdao Teachers' College.

Tomb of Kang Youwei The tomb was reconstructed in 1985 at the southern side of Fushan Mountain. On the tombstone is an epitaph composed by Liu Haisu, a contemporary master painter and one of Kang's disciples.

Fushan Mountain As the southwestern extension of Laoshan Mountain, it is 5km long east-west and 2km wide north-south, with a summit of 369 meters. During the foggy season, the mountain peaks seem as if they were floating on a sea of cloud. Plans are under way to build an eco-based entertainment park here.

Opposite: Sketch map of the eastern part of the city (continued)
Below: Music Square

Qingdao Municipal Museum The Museum at 27 Meiling Road has the largest showroom in Shandong Province, staging historical and contemporary exhibitions on a regular basis, such as the Qingdao International Animation Show.

Polar Ocean World With more than 10,000 ocean creatures on show, the newly-opened Polar Ocean World houses over 200 polar animals such as beluga, penguin, polar bear, sea otter and walrus in a total area of 210,000m². Stunt shows are staged daily at regular intervals every day.

Qingdao Seaside Sculpture Museum Between the sea and

Donghai Road, this museum has an indoor section and an outdoor one – a unique picturesque view with sculptures silhouetted against the sky and sea.

Haier Sci-tech Museum Next to Qingdao Municipal Museum, Sci-tech is the only museum nationwide run by a business entity based in Qingdao: Haier, a white goods giant in China.

Qingdao International Beer City The 35-hectare Beer City falls into two parts of trade and entertainment, where many brands of beer and snacks are offered, along with drinking contests and amusement shows. Built in 1993 and ranked one of the first 43 national tourist attractions, it is set to become the permanent site for the Qingdao Beer Festival. Hailed as Qingdao's Disneyland, it introduced Carnival in 2004.

Below: Polar Ocean World
Opposite top-down:
International Beer City
International Golf Course
Etsong Stadium
Qingdao International Convention Center

Qingdao International Golf Course The 999,000m² course in High-tech Park was designed according to international standards – 18 holes, par 72.

Haier Industrial Park A tour of this industrial park will reveal the white goods manufacture and corporate culture of Haier Group.

Etsong Stadium This is a spectacular sports stadium with a capacity of 60,000 people.

Qingdao International Convention Center Largest of its kind in Shandong

Province, the Center in Miaoling Road stages grand exhibitions such as the China International Consumer Electronics Show (SINOCES) and Qingdao International Fashion Week.

Shilaoren (Old Stone Man) One hundred meters offshore is a huge rock formation shaped like the bust of an old man – a symbol of the Shilaoren National Holiday Resort since 1992.

Rain Forest Valley Built in conformity with the natural landscape inside Shilaoren National Holiday Resort, it is noted for the birds' stunt in the tropical rain forest, and an eco-show featuring such animals as tigers from Northeast China, South China and Bengal.

Shilaoren Sight-seeing Park On the way to Laoshan Mountain, this park is a haven for people who wish to shun the bustling city by experiencing farm work and agricultural customs.

Other Tourist Attractions

Beach Combing at Hongdao Fish bait, fishing rods and roasting kits for anglers and fun-seekers are provided in a beach of 79,920m² area in Hongdao, Chengyang District.

Chengyang Century Park Measuring 429,570m², the Park in Chengyang District is designed in the

manner of Suzhou Garden in South China's Jiangsu Province.

Children's Park An amusement park on Zhushuishan Hill, literally meaning water-storage, used to be a site for storing water during the German Occupation period one century ago. Now it is the site for the annual Radish Festival in the first month of the Chinese lunar year.

TCM Sculpture Park in Nanshan Hill The Green-covered Nanshan Hill on Anshan 2nd Road is dedicated to the accomplishment of TCM, presenting the statues of Li Shizhen (1518-1593) and Sun Simiao (581-682) – both are ancient TCM experts – as well as sculptures of human body organs and acupuncture points.

Tsingtao Beer Museum The first beer museum in China, it is housed in Tsingtao Beer Brewery, at 56 Dengzhou Road. Visitors will be enlightened about the origin, development and brewing of Tsingtao beer while sampling fresh beer of various tastes.

Tsingtao Beer Street Bars and restaurants line this 800-meter-long Street of European style, in front of the Tsingtao Brewery on Dengzhou Road.

Shimei'an Park Some 4,000 flower trees make Shimei'an the largest garden of plum blossoms in North China. Chinese calligraphic works on plum blossoms, engraved by Xiu De (1920-1992), are on display.

Phoenix Island This Island in Huangdao District resembles a phoenix spreading its wings. Otherwise named Xuejia Island (Island of the Xues) after Xue Lu, a General of the Ming Dynasty, it boasts both Golden Beach and Silver Beach, accessible by bus and ferry.

Zhucha (Bamboo Fork) Island Known as "the Jewel of the Yellow Sea", the 1.03km^2 island off the coast of the Phoenix Island is a favorite haunt of anglers.

Liansan (Linking Three) Islands Three small islands of 1.6km^2, linked by low tide and separated by high tide, are home to rare aquatic products.

Qi Great Wall The beacon tower named Old Dragon Head with a height of 22 meters and an area of

Opposite above: Chengyang Century Park
Opposite below: Rain Forest Valley
Above: Tsingtao Beer Street
Below: Tsingtao Beer Museum

Above: Qi Great Wall

3,571m², is located at the eastern end of the Great Wall in Huangdao District. It was built by the Qi State in the Spring and Autumn Period.

Xiaozhushan Mountain The 104km² mountain along the coast of the Development Zone is a National Forest Park, containing some constructions of historical significance, such as Zhaoyang Temple and Baiyun Temple. Some remains of the Qi Great Wall remind people of this military fortress in ancient times.

Wild Animal Park A number of wild animals are kept at the Park in Xiaozhushan Mountian.

Mahao Canal Ruins Park The ruins of an ancient canal on the present Changjiang Road in Huangdao District has been transformed into a park, in which a small part of the Canal is maintained.

Golden Beach Southeast of Phoenix Island (Xuejia Island) in Huangdao District, Golden Beach has incomparable fine and vast sand.

III. Laoshan Mountain

A Famous Mountain on the Sea

Literally referring to the vastness of the boulders and the painstaking effort of climbing, Laoshan Mountain was named in the Tang Dynasty thanks to the boom of Taoism.

Approved as one of the first National Parks in 1982, Laoshan Mountain is a household name for the sea and mountain as well as the Taoism shrine.

As one of the cradles of Chinese Taoism since the Spring and Autumn Period, Laoshan Mountain has been hailed as the shrine of Taoism, attracting pilgrims and tourists from home and abroad.

Buddhism in Laoshan Mountain can also be traced back to ancient times as represented by Huayan Temple and Fahai Temple.

About 40km from the downtown area, Laoshan Mountain is accessible via three land routes involving the southern, eastern and central parts of the Mountain.

Because of the traffic, it is customary for travel agencies to take the southern route that covers both the Jufeng Peak and Taiqing Palace. The Laoshan Mountain stands out spectacularly when the tourists are riding between the steep cliff above and the wavy sea below,

It is hardly possible for tourists to cover all the scenic spots in the vast Laoshan Mountain in a short period of time. The more routes taken, the less regret remains.

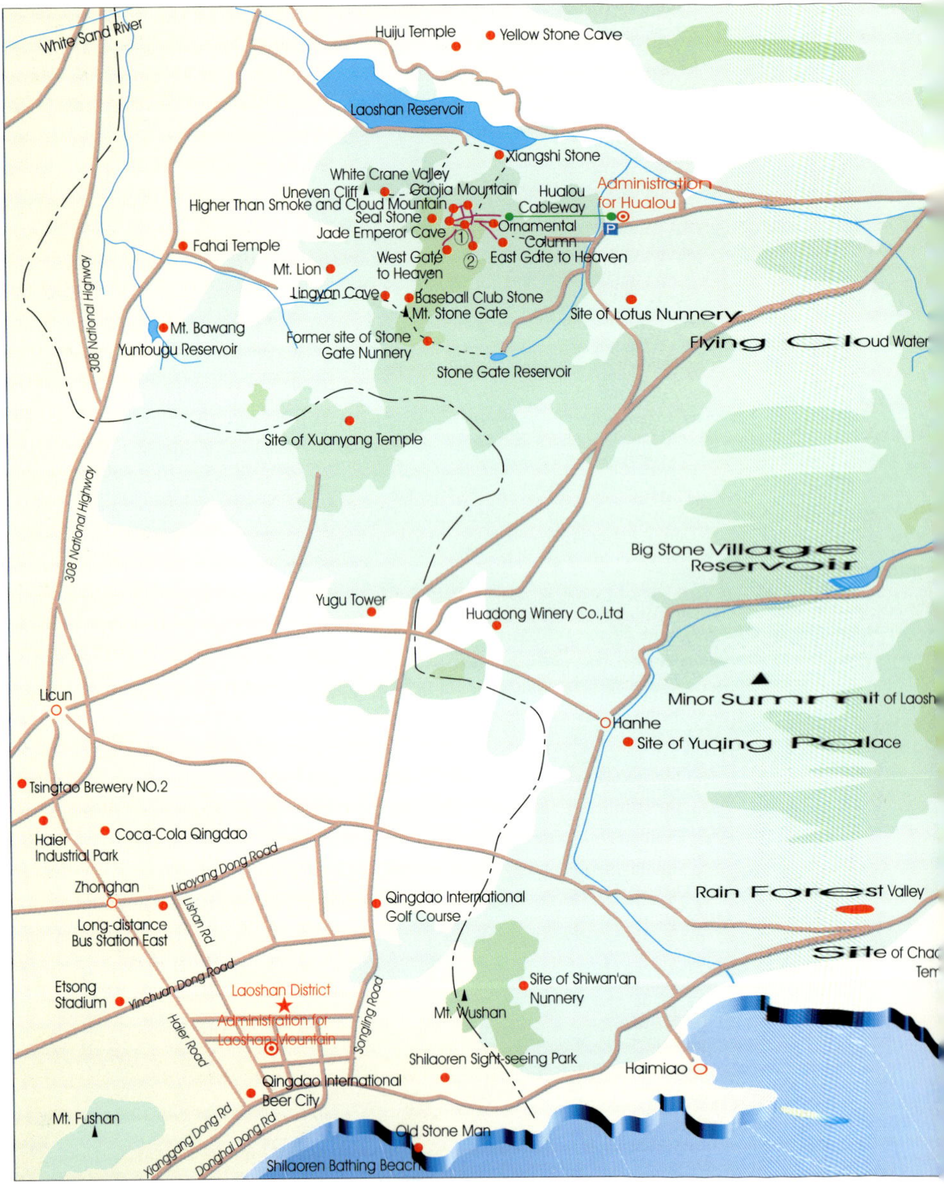

Sketch Map of Scenic Spots in Laoshan Mountain

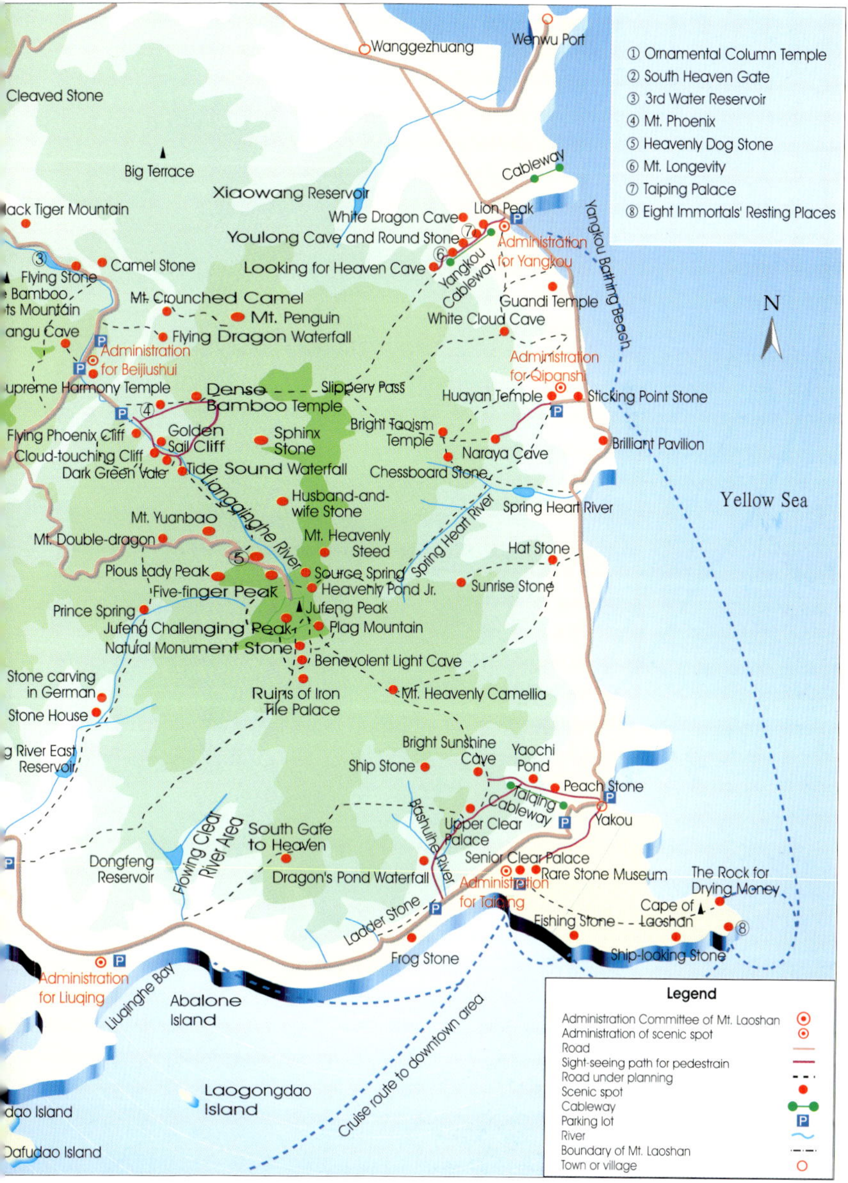

① Ornamental Column Temple
② South Heaven Gate
③ 3rd Water Reservoir
④ Mt. Phoenix
⑤ Heavenly Dog Stone
⑥ Mt. Longevity
⑦ Taiping Palace
⑧ Eight Immortals' Resting Places
N
Yellow Sea
Wanggezhuang
Wenwu Port
Cleaved Stone
Big Terrace
Xiaowang Reservoir
Cableway
Lion Peak
White Dragon Cave
Youlong Cave and Round Stone
Administration for Yangkou
Yangkou Cableway
Yangkou Bathing Beach
Camel Stone
Flying Stone
Looking for Heaven Cave
Mt. Crounched Camel
Mt. Penguin
Guandi Temple
White Cloud Cave
Flying Dragon Waterfall
Administration for Beijiushui
Administration for Qipanshi
Dense Bamboo Temple
Slippery Pass
Huayan Temple
Sticking Point Stone
Flying Phoenix Cliff
Golden Sail Cliff
Sphinx Stone
Bright Taoism Temple
Brilliant Pavilion
Cloud-touching Cliff
Dark Green Vale
Tide Sound Waterfall
Naraya Cave
Chessboard Stone
Lianggianghe River
Husband-and-wife Stone
Spring Heart River
Mt. Yuanbao
Mt. Double-dragon
Mt. Heavenly Steed
Hat Stone
Pious Lady Peak
Source Spring
Heavenly Pond Jr.
Sunrise Stone
Five-finger Peak
Jufeng Peak
Prince Spring
Jufeng Challenging Peak
Flag Mountain
Natural Monument Stone
Benevolent Light Cave
Stone carving in German
Ruins of Iron Tile Palace
Mt. Heavenly Camellia
Stone House
River East Reservoir
Bright Sunshine Cave
Yaochi Pond
Ship Stone
Peach Stone
Taiqing Cableway
Yakou
Upper Clear Palace
Baishuihe River
South Gate to Heaven
Flowing Clear River Area
Dongfeng Reservoir
Senior Clear Palace
Rare Stone Museum
The Rock for Drying Money
Dragon's Pond Waterfall
Administration for Taiqing
Cape of Laoshan
Ladder Stone
Fishing Stone
Ship-looking Stone
Frog Stone
Administration for Liuqing
Liuqinghe Bay
Abalone Island
Cruise route to downtown area
Laogongdao Island
dao Island
Dafudao Island
Legend
Administration Committee of Mt. Laoshan
Administration of scenic spot
Road
Sight-seeing path for pedestrain
Road under planning
Scenic spot
Cableway
Parking lot
River
Boundary of Mt. Laoshan
Town or village

Above: Sunset at Bashui River
Opposite: Flower-covered mountains in spring

fully demonstrating the charm of the "Mountain on the Sea".

The eastern route to Yangkou Beach, covering Taiping (Peace) Palace and Qipan (Chessboard) Stone Area, is an ideal place to appreciate the sunrise on the sea.

The central route to Beijiushui (North Nine Waters) unfolds the tranquilly beautiful picturesque landscape.

Laoshan Mountain has nine tourism areas: Jufeng (the Peak), Dengying Village, Liuqing River, Taiqing Palace, Shangqing Palace, Qipan Stone, Yangkou Beach, Beijiushui and Hualou Mountain.

While some scenic spots remain inaccessible deep in the mountains, Jufeng Peak is accessible by way of Dahedong.

Proposed Itineraries in Laoshan Mountain

Route A (southern route): Bashui (Eight Waters) River, Longtan (Dragon's Pond) Waterfall and Xiaqing (Lower Clear) Palace

Route B (Jufeng Peak route): Dahedong (Big River East) and Jufeng

Route C (eastern route): Taiping Palace, Mitian (Looking for Heaven) Cave, Yangkou Beach (Huayan Temple could be covered if the tourists drive by themselves).

Route D (central route): Beijiushui, Weizhu (Dense Bamboo) Temple and Chaoyin (Tide Sound) Waterfall (Also known as the northern route. Hualou Mountain could be covered if time is sufficient).

One-day trip to Laoshan Mountain can be reserved at hotels, which mostly follow the southern and central routes. Tourists are advised to confirm the ticket prices of Laoshan Mountain before boarding the tour buses. Self-help tours to Laoshan Mountain can also be achieved by taking public buses that start from the Railway Station, Tuandao, Taidong or Licun. The bus numbers are as follows: 110 (Taidong-Beijiushui), 104 (Taidong-Liuqing River), 304 (Ferry-Yakou), 311(Railway Station-Beijiushui), 365 (Dagang 2nd Road), 802 (Railway Station-Yakou).

The Southern Route

Dengying Scenic Area

The first landscape that comes into view in this Village on the way to Laoshan Mountain is the precipitous bluff popping up on the left, and the deep and serene sea rippling on the right. A tour in spring would promise an even more captivating view with the florescent snow-white pear blossoms.

Jufeng Scenic Area

Centering on an area of 7.4km² of apexes and forests, Jufeng Peak is accessible either on foot or by car (or cable car) from all sides, although it is hard to scale. Here are some routes for climbers to follow.

The southern route: Chartered bus service at Dahedong → Entrance to the Peak → Cable car or hiking to the Peak

The eastern route: Shangqing Palace or Mingxia (Bright Sunshine) Cave → Jufeng Peak

The western route: Hanhe → Shibapan (Eighteen Mountian Bends) → Liushutai (Willow Mountain) → Shang Shibapan →Jufeng Peak

The northwestern route: Yulinkou (Fish Scale Pass) → 5km climbing → Jufeng Peak

The northern route: Weizhu Temple → Mingdaoguan (Bright Taoism) Temple → Hualiukou (Slippery Pass) → Jufeng Peak

Jufeng Peak The 1,133-meter-high Jufeng Peak tops all the mountains scattered along the 18,000km coastline in China. Four views are typical of the Jufeng Peak: Laoshan fireball, miracle of cloud sea, Jufeng Peak silhouetted against the rising sun, and silver mountains mantled in sleet.

Above: Cloud sea at Laoshan Mountain
Below: Bigaogu
Opposite: Qiannu Peak

Bagua (Eight Diagrams) Gate Experts on I-Ching

Studies designed the Eight Diagrams Gate based on the eight mountain passes around Jufeng Area, which asserts the harmonious coexistence of heaven, earth and human.

Shang Shibapan (Upper Eighteen Mountain Bends) Claiming the unrivaled height of all the mountain motorways, this is the only way to Jufeng along the western route. It takes one hour by car and five hours on foot to reach Jufeng Peak.

Huangye (Yellow Leaves) Peak The 840-meter-high mountain is covered with larches that turn yellow in autumn. Rare plants such as bracken grow in spring and pine-mushroom in autumn.

Heifengkou (Dark Wind Pass) When hiking to Jufeng, one will confront an 871-meter-high ridge where wind howls through the pass, causing capricious weather in summer.

Qiannu (Pious Lady) Peak The lady-like rock formation seems to be worshipping God on a mountain top near the road to Jufeng Peak.

Wuzhi (Five-finger) Peak Resembling five fingers, the two 1,050-meter-high mountain ranges of Jufeng Peak pierce the sky.

Bigaogu (Jufeng Challenging) Peak Looking as high as Jufeng Peak, the mountain alongside Jufeng Peak commands such a superb view of the whole city that even the west bank of Jiaozhou Bay is in sight.

Lingqi (Flag) Mountain Like a flaunting flag, this Mountain, southeast of Jufeng Peak, is the second highest peak in Laoshan Mountain.

A Seam of Sky A huge boulder adjacent to the south of Jufeng Peak has a one-meter-wide and 20-meter-high crevice in the center, through which a seam of sky is in view.

Ziranbei (Natural Monument) Stone A monument-like stone south of the piedmont of Jufeng Peak forms a 24-meter-high and 8-meter-wide crude cuboid, glittering in the sun.

Ciguangdong (Benevolent Light) Cave The egg-shaped cave to the southwest of Ziran Monument was excavated in a huge boulder in the mid-Yuan Dynasty (1206-1370) for cultivation of the Taoist doctrine.

Tianyi Spring Situated north of Jufeng Peak, Tianyi Spring is famous for its highest location among all the springs of Laoshan Mountain. A conflux of streams, it is the source of the Chaoyin Waterfall and Baishahe (White Sand) River.

Jufengkou (Jufeng Pass) To the southeast of Jufeng Peak stands a cove where a unique view of the neighboring mountains is secured. Further south of Jufeng Pass stands Diaoyutai, a protruding rock formation well-suited for fishing, weather permitting.

Hualiukou (Slippery Pass) As a major pass and range in the northern part of Jufeng Area, Hualiukou is thus named due to its slippery paths.

Historical and Cultural Corridor An 8-kilometer-long wall decorated with embossed patterns about Taoism and Chinese Boxing, which will accompany the tourists who enter Laoshan Mountain.

Ruins of Tiewa (Iron Tile) Palace Built during the reign of Emperor Jiajing (1522-1566) of the Ming Dynasty, this highest temple of Taoism in Laoshan Mountain was

later burned in a forest fire, leaving nothing more than 10 stone pillars.

Liuqing (Flowing Clear) River Scenic Area

In the center of the river mouth stands Laogong Island. Baoyu (Abalone) Island, a peninsula in which abalone breed, is on one side of the bay. Other scenic spots include the Reservior of Liuqing River, Jiangjun (Military General) Trough Reservoir and Tizi (Ladder) Stone.

Shangqing Scenic Area

This area features the Shangqing Palace and Mingxia Cave as well as the Bashui (Eight Waters) River and Longtan Waterfall. Safety is the top priority in touring this area during flood season, when torrents are likely to break out.

Below: Shangqing Palace
Opposite above: Ziranbei Stone
Opposite below: Liuqing river mouth

Mingxia (Bright Sunshine) Cave As the first temple of Taoism in Laoshan Mountain, the 2-meter-high cave has $10m^2$ floor area, with a roof of yellow glazed tiles glistening in the rays of sunlight.

Shangqing (Upper Clear) Palace Built in the year 960, about 1.5km south of Mingxia Cave, the Palace was once the leading shrine of Taoism in Laoshan Mountain, following Taiqing Palace.

Longtan (Dragon's Pond) Waterfall Not far from the south of Shangqing Palace, Longtan Waterfall pours like a Jade Dragon from the

20-meter-high cliff. Torrents are expected during the raining season.

Taiqing Scenic Area

Commanded by Taiqing Palace, this area also contains such scenic spots as Yakou (the Pass), Diaoyutai (Fishing Stone), Baxiandun (Eight Immortals' Resting Places) and Laoshantou (Cape of Laoshan Mountain). It is here that the earliest temple garden in Laoshan Mountain was conceived, considered a subdivision of the ancient Chinese garden system.

Above: Longtan Waterfall
Opposite: Taiqing Palace

Taiqing (Senior Clear) Palace As the premier and the earliest temple of Taoism in Laoshan Mountain, as well as the second woods of the Taoist Quanzhen Sect, this Palace falls into three temple clusters: Sanguan (Three Officials), Sanqing (Three Clears) and Sanhuang (Three Emperors).

Sanguan Hall Styled in the then-prevailing architecture of the Song Dynasty (960 – 1279), this Hall is the oldest Taoist temple in Laoshan Mountain, where officials of Heaven, Earth and Water are worshipped. Numerous ancient trees grow here such as the 2,100-year-old sabina chinerisis and the 1,000-year-old gingko. The 600-year-old camellia (cold-resistant) is one of the rarest, described as Crimson Snow by Pu Songling in *Xiangyu* collected in his *Liao Zhai Zhi Yi (Strange Stories of Liao Zhai)*.

Sanqing Hall As the second hall cluster of the Taiqing Palace, Sanqing Hall has one major hall and two side halls. In the major hall the three Gods of Sanqing (Three Clears) are worshipped; in the Eastern Hall Emperor Donghua is worshipped, and the West Hall is for Wang Mu Niang Niang (Queen Mother of the West).

Memorial for Guan Yu and Yue Fei Two military generals of ancient China: Guan Yu (160 – 219) and Yue Fei (1103 – 1141), are worshipped in the Memorial to the west of Sanqing Palace. The ruins of the wall in the courtyard is said to be the wall the generals magically passed through without injuring themselves.

Sanhuang (Three Emperors) Hall In the rectangular compound to the west of Sanqing Palace, three emperors of Heaven, Earth and Human are worshipped, along with the ten renowned TCM doctors of ancient times. In the courtyard grows a three-in-one tree of ancient cypress, trumpet creeper and Chinese sumac sharing the same trunk.

Kangcheng Academy of Classical Learning Formerly the Showroom of Laoshan Rare Stone in Taiqing Scenic Area, it is now an Academy for Chinese classical learning, run jointly by the local administration and Shandong University.

Taiqing Bay Tourists who take the cruise route disembark here, opposite Taiqing Palace. This acclaimed moonlit bay is ranked one of the best scenes of Laoshan Mountain.

Diaoyutai (Fishing Stone) Eastward of Taiqing Bay, Diaoyutai Stone projects beyond the sea. With its flat and spacious surface, the Stone is an ideal place for fishing.

Baxiandun (Eight Immortals' Resting Places) Dozens of rocks in various colors and sizes are set against

the corroded cliff, otherwise dubbed "Cape of Laoshan Mountain", to the east of Taiqing Bay. They are said to be the resting places for the legendary Eight Immortals before they set off on their trans-oceanic journey.

The Eastern Route

Yangkou Scenic Area

Backed by the mountains and facing the sea eastward, the Area boasts an unparalleled sunrise view. Places of Taoism interest include Taiping (Peace) Palace, Bailong (White

Dragon) Cave, Youlong Cave, Baiyun Cave and Guandi Temple. Some mountain landscapes and seascapes of Yangkou Bay are accessible by cableway from Yangkou Hotel to Mitian (Looking for the Heaven) Cave. A merrymaking chute and the bathing beach add to the fun of Yangkou Bay.

Taiping Palace Climbing some 500 meters to the west of Yangkou Bay, one would end up in this Taoist Palace, built in the early Song Dynasty. In the western courtyard gushes Longxian (Dragon Saliva) Spring. The morning toll of the bronze Eight-Diagram Bell in the eastern courtyard is one of the enchanting scenes of Laoshan Mountain.

Sheep Stone This stone resembles a sheep grazing amid the trees outside the eastern courtyard of Taiping Palace.

Lion Peak Looking like a fierce lion commanding the sea below, the Peak is looked upon as God's bestowal upon man for sunrise appreciation. More than 10 people can be accommodated either on its neck or back.

Youlong Cave and Hunyuan (Round) Stone Behind Taiping Palace, a cave naturally formed with three huge rocks has the capacity of 20 to 30 people, the top of which is a round stone engraved Hunyuan (Round) Stone.

Mitian (Looking for Heaven) Cave One may hike or take the cableway from behind Taiping Palace to reach the Cave,

Opposite above: Baxiandun
Opposite below: Yangkou Bathing Beach
Below: Taiping Palace

whose exploration is absolutely risky and fascinating, particularly with candle or torch in hand.

Shangyuan (Upper Garden) Mountain A huge stone dubbed Turtle Belly tops the Mountain, from which a view of the various boulders in the distance is secured.

Baiyun (White Cloud) Cave Hiking by way of Diaolongzui (Eagle Dragon's Beak) south of Yangkou, followed by escalating steps to the west, will lead you to the 400-meter-high cave. Built in 743 of the Tang Dynasty for religious purposes, it was re-designed into a Taoism temple by Tian Baiyun, a Taoist of Laoshan Mountain. Supported by three huge rocks, the major hall is 15-16 meters in both depth and width, accommodating dozens of people. The Cave and the ancient pine trees growing behind it constitute a landscape painting, enhanced by 200-year-old magnolia, as well as century-old pawpaw and chestnut.

Daxian (The Primary Immortal) Mountain and Erxian (The Secondary Immortal) Mountain Side by side on the southeast of Baiyun Cave, Daxian Mountain is unattainable, while Erxian Mountain can be reached by Shangtianti (Ladder Ascending the Heaven) where immortals are supposed to be waiting at Huixiantai (Immortals Meeting Mountain). Two stone towers housing the remains of the Taoists were erected in the Peripatetic Valley, a fairly level and beautiful valley between the two mountains.

Guandi Temple The oldest and largest temple of its kind in Qingdao, and situated at the foot of Shangyuan Mountain to the southwest of Yangkou Bay, Guandi (Guan Yu, a general of ancient times) Temple was built during the reign of Emperor Wanli (1573 – 1619) of the Ming Dynasty.

Qipan Stone Scenic Area

Accessible from both Yangkou eastward and Yakou southward, the Area is dotted by Qipan Stone, Naraya Cave, Mingdaoguan and the Huayan Temple (of Buddhism), as well as some natural scenes of Dizhu Stone, Yugu Stone, Quanxin River Reservoir, Riqi (Sunrise) Stone, Gaoshi (High Stone) Hut, Tiancha Summit and Feiran Pavilion.

Dizhu (Sticking Point) Stone The largest stone inscription of Laoshan Mountain since ancient times has been credited to *Spectacle of the Mountains* *and Sea,* carved in a huge stone near Fanlinghou Village. Calligraphed by the provincial governor of Shandong in the Qing Dynasty, each of the four characters measures three meters in height.

The Statue of Yu Qi On the south of Dizhu (Sticking Point Stone) is a Statue of Yu Qi, leader of the local farmers' uprising in the early 17th Century. Yu Qi later became the Buddhist abbot of Huayan Temple and the founder of Mantis Boxing.

Huayan Temple Built during the reign of Emperor Shunzhi (1644-1661) of the Qing Dynasty, the Temple is one of the few Buddhist temples in Laoshan Mountain. With a floor area of 200m^2 in a 4,000m^2 premise, it mainly has three halls —— the first as the monks' living quarters, the second as Cangjingge (House for Buddhist Classics Collection), the third for worshipping Sakyamuni.

Naraya Cave Some 500 meters west of Huayan Temple is the Yugu (Fishing Drum) Stone with a hole in the center. Hiking a further 1.5km, one would confront the natural cave, 7 meters wide and 15 meters high and

Below: Autumn at Huayan Temple

Above: Qipan Stone

deep, with a hole on the top said to lead to Heaven. As one of the best scenes of Laoshan Mountain, it is the second largest cave in the world, as indicated in ancient religious books and records.

Statue of Fa Xian The Statue at the foot of Huayan Temple Mountain was built in commemoration of Fa Xian, a Buddhist dignitary who settled at Laoshan Mountain in the Eastern Jin Dynasty (317-420).

Wanghaimen (The Gate for Appreciating the Sea) Adjacent to Naraya Cave is Kunlun Mountain, topped by the 700m^2 Tianbo (Heavenly Wave) Pond. The Gate framed by three boulders is discernable from the neighboring mountains.

Mingdaoguan (Bright Taoism) Temple The 830-meter-high Temple on Zhaofeng Ridge, to the west of Wanghai Gate, tops all the religious buildings in Laoshan Mountain. Built during the reign of Emperor Kangxi (1662 – 1722) of the Qing Dynasty, it is a shrine where the Jade Emperor and Sanqing (Three Clears) are worshipped. Three gingko trees outside the courtyard are all more than 1,000 years old. Two naturally formed caves nearby — Tianran (Inartificial) and Sanzhen (Three Truths) were for Taoists' self-cultivation; they served as burial places for the remains of the deceased.

Tiancha (Heavenly Camellia) Summit A camellia hundreds of years old grows in the crevice of the eastern cliff of this mountain, located to the south of Mingdaoguan.

Qipan (Chessboard) Stone Some 500 meters south of Mingdaoguan, protrudes obliquely a 10-meter-long stone carved with a chessboard, where a dozen people can be accommodated. The legend that immortals once played chess here ranks the stone one of the best scenes of Laoshan Mountain.

Quanxin (Spring Heart) River "Heart" refers to the whirlpool conjoined by four brooks obstructed by a boulder in a vale north of Tiancha Summit. Named after the whirlpool, part of the river is turned into a reservoir that overflows in the summer, forming a waterfall.

Feiran (Brilliant) Pavilion The 1.7-meter-high and 1.2-meter-wide Pavilion in Fanlinghou Village is all made of stones — a perfect belvedere, small as it is.

The Central Route

Beijiushui Scenic Area

Beijiushui (North Nine Waters) originates in Tianyi Spring, the highest one in Laoshan Mountain. The influx of water ranges northwestward through the vales, forming a picturesque landscape, divided into nine reaches. This view of quiet and deep vales with clear, rippling water running through differs from the southern and eastern routes that feature mountains and the sea — this is a refreshing scene for the tourists.

Beijiushui (North Nine Waters) fall into Inner (Upper Reaches) Nine Waters and Outer (Lower Reaches) Nine Waters.

Outer Nine Waters The lower reaches of the river start from Juwan (Chrysanthemum Cove) east of Sunjiacun Village, and continue through Yusun (Jade Bamboo Shoots) Mountain and Heihu (Black Tiger) Mountain. The Sanshui (the Third Water) Reservoir is set against Jinping (Bright Screen) Rock. Further upward is Wushui (the Fifth Water), represented by Yusheng

(Reed Pipe) Vale, otherwise known as Huancui (Green) Vale. Liushui (the Sixth Water) is marked by Yingzhao (Eagle Claw) Pond under Yingzui (Eagle Beak) Mountain, with Luotuotou (Camel Head) Mountain ahead. Above Qishui (the Seventh Water) Village is Songtao (Pine Wave) Vale — Bashui (the Eighth Water).

Taihe (Supreme Harmony) Temple The temple, built in 1459 in the Ming Dynasty, was transformed into Jiushui Restaurant after being damaged in the Cultural Revolution of the 1960s. The temple commands a panorama of the Outer Nine Waters.

Nine Bends and Eighteen Ponds Eighteen ponds of different sizes and depths are built at various levels of the nine reaches, depending on the physical features of the landscape. The concept of conforming to nature, proposed by ancient Chinese philosophers Laozi and Zhuangzi (369BC – 295BC), is reflected in the names of each pond, given by Fan Zeng (1938 –), an eminent contemporary Chinese painter.

Neiyishui (The Inner First Water) Water overflows the bridge. Clear brooks feed into a deep and serene pond, upon which the bright moon is reflected in the moonlit nights.

Nei'ershui (The Inner Second Water) Water courses through Shuangshiwu Village (Double Stones House Village) where the General Mountain is in view.

Neisanshui (The Inner Third Water) Split into fine streams by huge rocks, the water splashes here like cascades, echoed by the precipice across the vale named Mini Stone Forest of Laoshan Mountain.

Neisishui (The Inner Fourth Water) Above the Yingchou (hard

for Eagle to cover) Canyon, the mountain crests rise so high that they seem to be cloud-kissing, jeopardized by Shimen (Stone Gate) Pavilion on the mountainside.

Opposite: Cascade
Above: One of 18 ponds at Beijiushui

Neiwushui (The Inner Fifth Water) On the southern bank of the rill towers Phoenix Bluff, with complicated and gorgeous veins on its surface. A phoenix on the wing is reflected in the water, viewed from an appropriate angle.

Neiliushui (The Inner Sixth Water) Led by the water, the stone path escalates and twists with the mountain range, with Jingtian (Mirror Heaven) Pond below and Jinfanzhang (Brocade) Cliff alongside, shining like a piece of brocade in the sun.

Neiqishui (The Inner Seventh Water) • Lengcui (Dark Green) Vale The dense pine trees growing on the bluffs along the Vale impart a dark green color to the water – golden in autumn with the yellow leaves and flowers. Tourists may be taken aback by a cleaver

The central route includes Beijiushui, and Hualou Scenic Areas, as well as the townships of Xifu, Beizhai and Xiazhuang.
Beijiushui is noted for Nine Bends and Eighteen Ponds, mixed with rushing riffles and quiet reaches, in the midst of magnificent rocks and mountains —Jiushui Gallery.

hanging overhead, described as something scary by General Zhu De (1886 – 1976).

Neibashui (The Inner Eighth Water) The water is surrounded by bluffs and rocks like city walls between Big Dragon Gate and Small Dragon Gate, leaving the sky above round in shape, ringed by yellow leaves in autumn.

Neijiushui (The Inner Ninth Water) • Fish Scale Vale Cobbles of various forms and sizes in the Vale look like scales of fish — alive in the rippling water.

Chaoyin (Tide Sound) Waterfall The Primary Waterfall in Laoshan Mountain drops so forcefully that it scours out a hole on the rock on its way to Diangang (Indigo Vat) Cove. A pavilion on the precipice north of the cove overlooks the Waterfall and the Cove.

Weizhu (Dense Bamboo)Temple Hiking northward from Sanshui (The Third Water), you will arrive at the temple, built on a 1,730 m^2 premise in the reign of Emperor Wanli (1573–1619) of the Ming Dynasty. It is surrounded by grotesque stones and rare plants, such as the century-old white clove and boxtrees.

Liushutai (Willow Mountain) Village 500 meters southwest of

Beijiushui is Guanlao (Overlooking Laoshan) Village, above which is Liushutai Village, the watershed between the South and North Jiushui Resort. The twisting downhill route to Hanhe Village is called Shibapan (Eighteen Bends), and the uphill route to Jufeng Peak is called Shang Shibapan (Upper Eighteen Bends). The Administration of Agriculture and Forestry was set up here during the German Occupation one century ago, along with an affiliated primary school. Tailiu Road, a road from Taidong (downtown) to the Village, was built at that time and is still in use today.

Opposite: Chaoyin Waterfall
Below: One bend at Beijiushui

Hualou Scenic Area

This is a mountainous area commanded by Hualou Peak, with Wulong (Five Dragons) Canyon to the east, Xiazhuang Village to the west, Laoshan Reservoir to the north, and Chahua (Camellia) Peak to the south.

Hualou (Ornamental Column) Peak Towering some 21 meters above the mountain, the square-surfaced Peak is composed of horizontal layers of rocks one on top of another. Looking like an ornamental column from the distance, it is one of the best scenes of Laoshan Mountain.

Hualou (Ornamental Column) Temple The Taoist Temple east of Hualou Peak was built in 1325 of the Yuan

Above: Weizhu Temple
Opposite: Distant view of Hualou Peak

Dynasty. Three gingko trees in the courtyard are 650 years old.

Biluo (Turquoise) Rock & Yuhuang (Jade Emperor) Cave Biluo Rock refers to a huge green-colored rock behind Hualou Temple under which is Yuhuang (Jade Emperor, the Supreme Deity of Taoism) Cave, a man-made elliptical cave where the Jade Emperor is worshipped.

Xiyang (Sunset) Canyon On the southwest slope of the Canyon below Hualou Temple, the bamboo grove, a rare strain of bamboo, takes on a unusually beautiful look in the afterglow.

Yingxian (Greeting Immortals) Stone North of Cuiping (Green Screen) Rock, a miniature cliff overhanging the path appears to be someone extending a greeting. To the west of it, Tianye (Heavenly Water)

Spring gurgles on the top of Dashi (Huge Stone) Peak, north of which Yunu (Fairy) Basin is discernible.

Lingyan (Higher Than Smoke and Cloud) Mountain A small mountian to the west of Yunu Basin, Lingyan is topped by a dozen potholes of various sizes, referred to as the Crystal Potholes.

Wuzu (Five Ancestors) Cave & Qizhen (Seven Quanzhen Disciples) Cave There are two caves east of Hualou (Ornamental Column) Temple. One worships Zhang Boduan (987–1082), founder of the South Sect of Taoism, and four of his followers; the other is for the North Seven Quanzhen Disciples of Wang Chongyang (1112–1170), originator of Quanzhen Taoism.

Nantian (South Heaven) Gate • Chongyang Cave A small man-made cave alongside the Nantian Gate used to worship Wang Chongyang.

Yuezikou (Crescent) Reservoir North of Hualou Mountain, the Reservoir, otherwise known as Laoshan Reservoir, is fed by Baisha (White Sand) River and Wulong (Five Dragons) River at a crescent-shaped canyon. Built in the 1950s, it has a capacity of 56,000,000m^3.

IV. Scenic Spots in Suburban Cities

Jimo City

As a satellite city of Qingdao, Jimo boasts the Laoshan Mountain in the south and the Yellow Sea to the east. It is at the center of the manufacturing base and city cluster of Shandong Peninsula, and one of the majors cities within the 30-minute economic rim of Greater Qingdao. With 1.09 million people in the 18 towns of the 1,780km^2 land area, Jimo also has one economic development zone and one holiday resort, both of which are at provincial-level.

The history of Jimo dates back to the Qin Dynasty over 2,000 years ago when Jimo County was founded, which later developed into a city in 596 AD of the Sui Dynasty.

Jimo is a transport hub traversed by the two railways of Qingdao-Jinan and Lancun-Yantai as well as three expressways of Jinan-Qingdao, Qingdao-Yinchuan and Urumqi-Weihai. The downtown Jimo area is 15 kilometers from Qingdao Airport and 40 kilometers from Qingdao Port. The two local ports of Aoshan and Nudao add to its three-dimensional transport network.

The 183-km-long coastline in Jimo accounts for

[Qingdao]

N
Dazeshan Mountain
Jiudian
Dazeshan Town
Laiyang City
Chanzhi Reservoir
ountain Stone Cultural Ruins
Zheng Wengong Shang-bei (Upper Stele) on Tianzhu Mountain
Laixi City
Cui Zifan Gallery
Crescent Lake Park
Laolongwan
Yunshan Mountain
Xu Fu Village
Baozhu Valley
Yunshan Town
Ningqi Tomb
Pingdu City
Kangwang Tomb
Xiaogu River
Mingcun
Lottie Moon Christian Constructions
Qianfo Pavilion
Guxian Town
Dagu River
Sanheshan Mountain
Site of Jimo Feudal City-state
Xiagezhuang
Jiangshan
Liaolan
Zhanggezhuang
Former site of Bull-burning Battle
Jiaolai River
Qingdao-Yinchuan Expressway
Tongjiang-Sanya Expressway
Zhangjiafang
Huashan Town
Lingshan Town
The Ancient City of Xiongyasuo
South Jiaolai River
Nancun Town
Lingshan Mountain
an-Qingdao Expressway
Wenchang Pavilion
Qingdao Garment Fair
Wenquan Town
Tianheng Town
Hot Spring Resort
Tomb of the Five Hundred Loyalists at Tianheng Islar
Mashan Stone Forest
Jimo City
Gaomi City
Lancun
Liucun Town
Madian
Liu Ruozhuo's Tomb
Aoshanwei Town
Heavenly Well Hill
Crane Mountain
Jiaozhuo City
Aoshantou
Chengyang District
Xifu Town
Dagu River
Airport
Wanggezhuang Town
Gao Fenghan Memorial
The cultural Ruins of Sanlihe
Yingfang
Hongdao
Baisha River
Licang District
Nandu
Laoshan Mountain
Jiaozhou Bay
Puji
Laoshan District
Shazikou
ear Moon Lake Forest Park
Aishan Mountain
Changmenyan Island
Downtown Qingdao
Shilaoren Holiday Resort
Ancient Horse Feedlot
Huangdao
The Great Wall of the Qi State
Huangdao District
Xiaozhushan Mountain
Zhuchadao Island
Phoenix Island
Phoenix Holiday Resort
Fengtai Town
Jiaonan City
Golden Beach
Tiejueshan Mountain
Dazhushan Town
The Yellow Sea
Dazhushan Mountain
Lingshan Island
Langya
Boli
Langyatai Holiday Resort
Crying Grave
Zhaitang Island
Vuguan Island

1/100 of the national total, off which the sea area covers 2,517km^2 containing abundant marine resources. Aoshan Bay is second to Jiaozhou Bay in Qingdao where resources are centralized such as mountain, sea, hot spring, island, beach and natural harbor. As a center of marine products and marine research in China, Jimo is developed in sea-farming industry providing fish and shellfish for high-end consumers in 24 islands and 17 reefs, which are also the dreamland for holiday makers.

The economy of Jimo is supported by the six industrial clusters of knit wear and accessories, business and trade, tourism, shipbuilding and spare parts, electronics and components, as well as food and beverage.

Mashan Stone Forest Mashan Mountain is 7km west of Jimo City. The peak is 211 meters high and its southwestern part is composed of dust-color andesite that features columnar jointing. The section of a single column is around one square meter and the column is as high as 30 meters. Viewed from the distance, these stone pillars look like a thick forest formed by the trees growing straight against each other. Mashan Mountain is also the home to the fossil wood that boasts the largest deposit nationwide.

Below: Mashan Stone Forest
Opposite: Sketch map of scenic spots in suburban cities

Heshan (Crane) Mountain Heshan Mountain is acclaimed as a supernatural shrine of Taoism as described by an ancient poem that goes like "The majestic height of Taishan Mountain is dwarfed by Laoshan

Mountain on the East China Sea, which is, though, dominated by the deiform Heshan Mountain".

A 10-meter-high boulder above the Yuzhen Palace resembles a crane combing its hair with its beak turning backward. The easiness and the serenity it reveals echoes the Taoist doctrine that advocates WU-WEI — a way of mastering circumstances by understanding their nature or principle before shaping one's outlook and actions in accordance with them.

Crane has long been considered a sacred bird in Chinese history incarnating longevity and a spirit free of the worldly thought. Pious pilgrims who clap their hands in front of Sanzhen Palace will be rewarded by the singing of cranes that sound as if it was from the heaven.

Other mysteries include the "Water-resounding Staircase" from Yuzhen Palace to Laojun Palace. With one person at the upper end of the staircase, the other one at the lower end would hear the chattering of the water, which seems as if it was given by God.

Changmenyan (Long Gate Rock) Island This 0.25km^2 Island off the coast of Aoshanwei Town, Jimo City, teems with Camellia — a tropical plant rarely seen in North China.

Liu Ruozhuo's Tomb Under municipal-level protection, the Tomb at the present Dongguan Primary School of Jimo City is in commemoration of Liu Ruozhuo, a Taoist dignitary in the Wudai Period (907 – 960).

Wenquan (Hot Spring) The Hot Spring Resort in Wenquan (Hot Spring) Town of Jimo City is the most frequented place in winter when waterborne recreations are limited. It is a 6.5 square kilometers area located in the suburb of Jimo, a satellite city and about 50 kilometers northeast of Qingdao City.

The hot spring is unique across the country in that the mineral water is free of sulphurated hydrogen as Wenquan Town is only three kilometers from the sea. The water tastes a bit salty and feels slippery, formed by the reverse flow of the seawater no more than 1,500 meters away from the sea.

The highest temperature is 93°C and the average temperature is 30°C-60°C. The water contains a number of elements such as salt,sulphur and bromine that help ease the ailments of skin problems, rheumatism, arthritis and early-stage cardiovascular diseases.

Traffic: Take Qingdao-Jimo long-distance bus and then transfer the bus to Fengcheng or Tianheng. Get off at Wenquan Town before arriving at either of the destinations.

Tips for skiing:
Outfit: warm, windproof and waterproof
Underwear: warm and of cotton material
Accessories: ski goggles, warm hat, non-slip gloves
Ski gear: ski shoes, ski boards and ski sticks

Tiantai Ski Resort Constructed in 2003 at Wenquan Holiday Resort, Jimo City, Tiantai Ski Resort is the first one of its kind in Shandong Province. It is 30 and 50 kilometers respectively away from Qingdao airport and the downtown Qingdao. Sit behind your wheel for 40 minutes and you will be at it if you take the Seaside Avenue from downtown Qingdao, which is usually packaged with the tour to Tianhengdao Island. In an area of 400 square kilometers, two ski slopes are unfolded that are 350-meter and 250-meter long respectively, along with the beginners' area and ski game entertainment area. With the snow machines imported from Canada, the ski resort remains snow-covered even though it doesn't snow. The whole set of the ski gear (ski shoes, ski boards and ski sticks, etc.) and 15 Mongolian yurts are for rent here, and a buffet

Opposite: Heshan Mountain
Below: Along the Moshui River

restaurant adds to the excitement of the snowfield.

Business hours is 8:30 – 20:30, December through February. Free shuttle buses are offered at Jusco, Xianggang Middle Road and Parkson, Zhongshan Road. If you drive on your own, take Songling Road, and pass through Beizhai and Pishikou before you arrive at Ski Resort. Alternative way: Qingdao-Yinchuan Expressway – Yantai-Qingdao Expressway – Wenquan Town – Ski Resort.

Qingdao Garment Fair The largest one of its kind in North China, it occupies a premise of 111,000m^2 and a building area of 103,000m^2. Some 1,000 proprietors, 500 agencies and 200 name brand suppliers are involved in the trade of over 2,800 kinds of garments and knit goods.

Below: Tianheng Island
Opposite above: Jimo County Yamen
Opposite below: Military fortress at Xiongyasuo

Agricultural Ecosystem Park The Park, south of the fly-over in Jimo Development Zone, is aimed at pilot projects and the demonstration of vegetable cultivation.

Holiday Resort at Tianheng Island Featuring Qi State Culture of the Warring States (403BC – 221BC) and island scenery, the resort, 3.5km east of Tianheng Town, Jimo City, has a mini-golf course, a shooting range and a children merrymaking playground, in addition to villa clusters. Bus service to Tianheng Island is offered in Tuandao, Qingdao.

Tomb of the Five Hundred Loyalists at Tianheng Island Accompanied by a 17-meter-high sculpture of Tianheng and his loyalists, the Tomb on the hillock of the 1.46km^2 island, is said to be the burial place of the 500 partisans loyal to the bygone Qi State, who, following the suicide of Tianheng (202BC), killed themselves after learning that they would be executed by the Emperor of the then newly-established Han Dynasty.

The Ancient City of Xiongyasuo This square-shaped city was built in the early Ming Dynasty for marine defense on the seashore of Fengcheng Town, Jimo City. It was used as a military fortress against Japanese invasion.

Tianjing (Heavenly Well) Hill The 81-meter-high hill, 5km east of downtown Jimo, is topped by a well, named Longchi (Dragon Pond), as well as a Dragon King Temple, built in the early Southern Song Dynasty.

Tianhou (Marine Goddess) Palace at Jinkou Dating back 230 years, the Palace boasts the largest of its kind in Shandong Province.

Twin Brick Pagodas Located in Qiji Town, Jimo City, the two ancient Pagodas, made of brick, feature exquisite craftsmanship.

Jimo County Yamen (Government Office in Feudal China) The well-protected Yamen has a history of over 640 years.

Lingshan Hill The 154-meter-high hill, 10km north of Jimo City sees a temple fair each year on April 15th of the Chinese lunar calendar.

Laixi City

At the hinterland of Shandong Peninsula and sandwiched by Qingdao, Weihai, Yantai and Weifang, Laixi has an area of 1,522 square kilometers and a population of 723,000. As one of China's top 100 county-level cities in the overall economic strength, it is also awarded by the country for its achievement in environmental protection, farming and water conservancy.

Above: Crescent Park at Laixi city
Opposite: Eggshell basalts

Within the one-hour Economic Rim of Qingdao, Laixi is 80 kilometers away from Qingdao Port, 110 kilometers from Qianwan Port and 60 kilometers from Qingdao Airport. It is considered a transport hub in Shandong Peninsula, traversed by the expressways of Tongjiang-Sanya, Yantai-Qingdao, Weifang-Laiyang, Weifang-Shijiu and the Jinan-Yantai Railway.

Laixi is rich in resources of minerals, farm produce and water. The proved mineral reserves of graphite, diophite, bentonite and gold have ranked Laixi a leading producer and exporter of graphite in China. Farm produce ranges from peanut, vegetable, fruit to livestock, of which the per capita peanut output tops the county-level cities in China with the annual export of 150,000 tonnes, accounting for 22% of the national total. Another champion, in the Province though, is gained from the annual production of 500,000 tonnes of meat, egg and dairy. Agriculture is dependent on the stable water supply that is secured by Chanzhi Reservoir (Laixi Lake), the largest of its kind in Shandong Peninsula with a capacity of 402 million cubic meters. A number of rivers and streams meander through the city such as Dagu River and Zhuhe River, sources of the Yuehu Lake (the Crescent Lake), a tourist destination featuring landscape of lakes and Chinese constructions.

With food processing taking the lead of Laixi's economy, other industrial clusters include textile and garment, electronics and communications, machinery, mineral exploitation and building materials, as well as rubber and chemicals. As the national demonstration area for standardized production of farm produce, Laixi is also one of China's top counties in food industry, supported by 517 large-scale food processors and the industrial chains of livestock farming including cow rearing and dairy, chicken farming and poultry, hog farming and pork products, as well as vegetable growing and its processing, fruit cultivation and its processing, peanut growing and its processing.

Crescent Lake Park After the fashion of a modern garden, the Park named after the crescent-shaped water body is easy to access in downtown Laixi City.

Chanzhi Reservoir Built in the 1950s and ranking the largest in Shandong Peninsula, the 41.6km^2 Reservoir is 10km northwest of downtown Laixi – a resort with a park and an aquarium inside.

Daqing (Large Green) Mountain The 81-hectare mountain covered by dense vegetation is a refreshing resort.

Cui Zifan Gallery The Gallery houses and showcases the works of Cui Zifan (1915 –), master of Chinese painting who is a Laixi native.

Jiaozhou City

Jiaozhou City ranks one of China's top 100 county-level cities in terms of overall economic strength, along with such national awards for environmental protection, clean city and the home to Chinese folk art. Jiaozhou has a population of 780,000 and 13 towns in a total area of 1,210 square kilometers. It is one of the first coastal cities in Shandong Province opened to the world in the late 1980s.

Historical record shows that human settled in Jiaozhou as early as 4,500 years ago, living on hunting, farming and fishing, which formed the Sanlihe cultural heritage in the Neolithic Age. Historically referred to as "Golden Jiaozhou", it used to be one of the five biggest trading ports and the only business port north of the Yangtze River during the Tang and Song dynasties. Thousands of years of history helped brew the unique folk arts of Jiaozhou Yangge (a folk dance) and Jiaozhou Maoqiang Opera that have been included on the List of China's Intangible Cultural Heritages.

The transport system in Jiaozhou extends to all directions through its seaport, airport and railway stations. It is traversed by four electric railways of Qingdao-Jinan, Jiaozhou-Xinyi, Jiaozhou-Huangdao and Qingdao-Jinan, and four expressways of Tongjiang-Sanya, Jinan-Qingdao, Qingdao-Lanzhou and Jiaozhou Bay. With no more than 30-minute drive to Qingdao Port, Qianwan Port and Qingdao Airport respectively, Jiaozhou deserves a transport hub linking the Peninsula with the rest of Shandong Province and the inland areas of China.

Jiaozhou has seven industrial clusters of auto and ship parts, boiler auxiliary equipments, household appliances and electronics, steel structure, light and textile industries, food processing, as well as wood furniture and kitchen-wares. The past decade has seen Jiaozhou ranking first in county-level cities of Shandong Province in terms of export earnings, contributed mostly by the industrial processing and logistics in the Jiaozhou Bay Economic Rim. So far as many as 11 of the Global Top 500 have made their investment here such as Emerson (USA), as well as a number of domestic

name brand businesses like Haier and CIMC.

The Cultural Ruins of Sanlihe Some 2,000 eggshell basalts, dating back 4,000 years, have been unearthed in an area of 50,000m^2 in Sanlihe Village, Jiaozhou City.

Ancient Horse Feedlot Referred to as the Horse-keeping City, the feedlot, 1.5km northwest of Licha Village, was built in the Han Dynasty; only the south gate still exists.

Gao Fenghan Memorial The Memorial, located in the northern Sanlihe Village, is in commemoration of Gao Fenghan, an artist in poetry, calligraphy and painting, in the Qing Dynasty.

Opposite: A bird's-eye view of Jiaozhou City
Above: Zheng Wengong Shang-bei on Tianzhu Mountain

Aishan Mountain This 229-meter-high mountain, located in southern Jiaozhou City, is the highest one in the city. The two peaks standing out in the eastern and western ends look like two ears of a person.

Chengyue (Clear Moon) Lake Forest Park The Park, in southwest Jiaozhou City, consists of Chengyue Lake, a 6,700,000m^2 orchard, and an eco-forest of the same size.

Pingdu City

As the largest county-level city in Shandong Province, Pingdu has an area of 3,176 square kilometers and a population of 1.36 million. Within the 1-hour drive Economic Rim of Qingdao, Pingdu is easily accessible for its places of interest such as Dazeshan Mountain, and Tianzhushan Stone Inscription which is acclaimed as the origin of Chinese calligraphy. Linking Shandong Peninsula with the interior China, Pingdu is developed in the road network formed by the expressways of Qingdao-Yinchuan, Tongjiang-Sanya, Weifang-Laiyang and Urumqi-Weihai.

Known as the hometown of grape, peanut and vegetable, Pingdu is registered in the Ministry of Agriculture as one of the 25 farm produce bases for commodity grains, quality fruit, top cotton and lean hogs. The meat supply of Pingdu ranks sixth nationwide and first in Shandong Province. In addition to the rich resource of graphite, the proved reserves in Pindu range from gold, iron, marble, granite, talcum to diopside.

The favorable environment for foreign investment in Pingdu has given rise to the boom of export-oriented economy which falls into five clusters of electronics and household appliance, food processing, rubber and chemicals, auto spare parts, as well as machinery and metal casting. The pilot project has been implemented for agricultural cooperation between China's Mainland and Taiwan Province, together with the establishment of the food processing zone of Qingdao City.

Pingdu has been honored the national model city for environmental protection and is one of the top 100 counties in overall economic strength in China after it has been developing sustainably and healthily. The local environment ranks it one of China's top 50 small and medium-sized cities regarding the investment prospect.

Yueshi (Mountain Stone) Cultural Ruins The Ruins in Dazeshan Town date back 3,500 to 3,900 years, as evidenced by the unearthed stoneware, pottery, bone implements and clam tools made by the Dongyi People, one of the ancient Chinese tribes that settled in the Qingdao Area some five to six thousand years ago.

Yunshan (Cloud) Mountain As one of the cradles of the Quanzhen Sect, the Mountain, 20km to the northeast of downtown Pingdu, was a holy land of Taoism in ancient times.

The Feudal City-state of Jimo in Ancient China This City in Guxian Town was built in the Spring and Autumn Period, prospered as one of the five city-states of the Qi State in the Warring States and eventually died out in the Eastern Han Dynasty (25AD-220AD).

Zheng Wengong Shang-bei (Upper Stele) on Tianzhu Mountain This classic calligraphic work is on the southern slope of Tianzhu (Heaven

Pillar) Mountain, 25km northwest of Pingdu City. The calligraphy was made by the Confucian scholar Zheng Daozhao (511AD) for Zheng Wengong, a prefect, about his official performance. The 3-meter-high and 1.5-meter-wide stele contains 881 Chinese characters, showcasing the transition of Chinese calligraphy from Seal Script to Chancellary Script. It has been under state-level protection since 1988.

Dazeshan Mountain Covering an area of 324km^2 in northern Pingdu City, the Mountain has over 2,000 hilltops with a 737m summit. The Buddhist Nunnery and the vineyard remain the tourist attractions apart from the Grape Festival and Stone Festival.

Hometown of Xu Fu, the Alchemist The present Xu Fu Village contains the residence ruins of Xu Fu, an alchemist of the Qi State in the Qin Dynasty. Xu Fu is noted for searching "immortal herbs" across the sea under the mandate of Qinshihuang, the First Emperor of China.

Qianfo (A Thousand Buddhas) Pavilion Built

Below: The downtown area of Pingdu City

downtown in the Ming Dynasty, the Pavilion was renovated in 1992.

Jiaonan City

To the west of Qingdao across the Jiaozhou Bay is Jiaonan City with a population of 811,000, an area of 1,846 square kilometers and a coastline of 131 kilometers. Its geographic location beyond the sea once alienated itself from Qingdao until recent years when efforts have been taken to develop it into a new economic center west of Qingdao coast. Up to the present it has been turned into one of the most dynamic and most habitable cities in Shandong Province.

Jiaonan deserves the reputation it enjoys as one of China's best tourist cities and hometown of China's modern folk painting. Both the landscape and the history are time-honored at Jiaonan, referred to historically as "The Place of Interest in East China". Scenic spots include Langyatai, Lingshan Island, Dazhushan Mountain and Xiaozhushan Mountain. In addition, it boasts the Venice in the Orient – the Water Town, and Dani Painters Village known as the top one of its kind north of the Yangtze River.

Below: Stele of Qin Dynasty at Langya Hill Opposite: Pagoda Forest at Shimen Temple

Forty kilometers away from Qingdao Airport, Jiaonan is well developed in transport system, meeting the national standard for the infrastructures. In its vicinity are Qingdao Bonded Area, Customs House of the Development Zone and Qianwan Port. Two expressways of Tongjiang-Sanya and Qingdao-Lanzhou pass through here, facilitating the development of Dongjiakou Port, one of the three new ports of Qingdao Port, backed by Huangdao-Rizhao Railway.

With the national awards for its landscaping,

environmental protection and ecological conservation, Jiaonan attaches importance to urban planning, stressing eco-based development of mountain, sea, city and green coverage. The urban area under planning has reached 384 square kilometers featuring the port in the east, industries in the north, intellectual in the south and tourism in the west.

The Ruins of Langya, an Ancient City The City, presently Langya Town, was a leading port of military significance during the Spring and Autumn Period of the Qi State. It later became the largest port of the Qin Dynasty. Despite the fact that the ruins of the city are few and far between, a cultural site of the Shang Dynasty (1600BC – 1046BC) can be observed at Dongzaohu in the eastern part of the Town.

Langya Hill The 183-meter-high Hill stands out 5km southeast of Langya Town. The group sculptures enact the farewell scene when Xu Fu, the alchemist, set sail for searching the immortal herbs across the sea under the mandate of Emperor Qinshihuang.

Zhaitang (Fast Hall) Island Legend states that Emperor Qinshihuang, the First Emperor of China in the Qin Dynasty (221BC – 207BC), fasted for the "immortal herbs" on this Island southeast of Langya Hill. Here, tourists can experience the fishermen's life style.

Muguan (Bathing Place for Court Officials) Island The 0.4km^2 Island is 15km off the coast of the ancient Langya Port. Legend has it that the entourage of Emperor Qinshihuang bathed here prior to searching for the "immortal herbs".

Kufen (Crying Grave) Between Langya Hill and Zhaitang Island, a cluster of grave-shaped rocks emerge at intervals of ebb tide. These rocks are said to have been left by the local people who lamented the failure of Xu Fu's test sail in search of immortal herbs.

The Great Wall of the Qi State Built by the Qi State in the Spring and Autumn Period and the Warring States, the Great Wall remains the best

Above: Distant view of Lingshan Island
Opposite: Qingdao International Airport

protected of its kind in China, dating back to the Qin Dynasty. The 55km Wall runs through seven towns and villages in Jiaonan City and Huangdao District, entering the sea at Yujiaxiahe Village. A bird's-eye view of the Wall can be commanded from the top of Xiaozhushan Mountain.

Dazhushan Mountain This Mountain, located in Dazhushan Town, is named after Zhu Zhong, an immortal of the Tang Dynasty who settled in this area. The top cultural relics include grottos and the Shimen (Stone Gate) Temple, built in the Jin Dynasty (1115-1234).

Lingshan Island This island is located off the southeastern coast of Jiaonan City. The island is as large as 7.28km^2, and the peak reaches 513.6 meters high. About 70% of the island is covered by the forest mixed with grotesque stones. It is like a picturesque painting that vividly tells the story about rocks, reefs, bays and seagulls.

V. Information

Transportation

The advantaged location by the seaside makes Qingdao one of the few cities in China that boast virtually all means of transportation in modern metropolis — undersea tunnel (under construction), highway, cross-sea bridge and ferry, in addition to the conventional means of air, train and bus.

The City Multi-media Information Island (CMII) is a kiosk available in public places that automatically provides interactive services and information including traffic, hotel, restaurant, weather report, tourism and house leasing etc. Tourists are free to enjoy the e-service that offers solutions to any questions arising during your travel in Qingdao.

Air Transportation

Qingdao Liuting International Airport, 32km from downtown, operates over 800 flights, passenger and cargo, domestic and overseas, to more than 50 cities in China and such international destinations as Tokyo, Osaka, Fukuoka, Seoul, Busan, Daegu, Paris (via Shanghai), Singapore, Bangkok and Frankfurt.

Tickets are offered at 29 Zhongshan Road and a number of ticket offices, which is being replaced by E-booking online.

An ID card or a passport

must be provided before buying tickets. The flight schedule and ticket prices are subject to seasonal changes.

Airport shuttle buses are offered at three terminals:

Bus 701: Hai Tian Hotel – Airport (every 30 minutes, 6:00 – 21:00)

Shuttle bus: Xiehe Huatian Hotel – Airport (every 1 hour, 5:30 – 17:30)

Shuttle bus: Sifang Hotel – Airport (every 1 hour, 6:00 – 18:00)

Ticket price: 15 yuan/person

Hotline for shuttle bus service: 96567

Ticket offices

Name	Address	Telephone
Shandong Airlines (SDA) Ticket Office	2 Fuzhou South Road	85737888
Eastern Airlines Hotel Ticket Office	16 Yan'erdao Road	85732400
CAAC Qingdao Terminal Ticket Office	29 Zhongshan Road	82895577
CAAC Qingdao Passenger Transport Center Ticket Office	30 Xianggang Middle Road	85775555
Qingdao Air Ticket Booking Center	3 Yuantou Road (Licang District)	87610000
ANA Qingdao Office	76 Xianggang Middle Road	85783311

Sea Transportation

As a natural deep-water port free of silt and freezing, Qingdao is a crucial seaport in China, having trade relations with over 450 ports of 130 countries and regions. It ranks among the first several seaports in China in terms of TEU throughput, boasting a transshipping hub across the country.

At present, Qingdao Port offers three international lines for passenger transportation.

Name of liner	Terminals	Day	Address	Telephone
Xiang Xue Lan	Qingdao- Inchon	Mon & Thur	6 Xinjiang Road	82825001
Utopia 3	Qingdao-Simonoseki	Thur		

Departure (Cangkou Station)				Arrival (Cangkou Station)			
Train Number	Departure time	Terminal	Arrival time	Train Number	Departure time	Terminal	Arrival time
N394	7:40	Xuzhou	17:18	5025	21:50	Heze	7:11
5026	8:35	Heze	18:45	1081	19:22	Taiyuan	8:21
K344	13:00	Nanchang	8:40	K343	17:01	Nanchang	10:53
1112	15:45	Hankou	11:16	2031	21:11	Zhengzhou	12:17
2032	17:20	Zhengzhou	7:33	1111	17:04	Hankou	13:13
1206	18:30	Dandong	18:18	1205	15:33	Dandong	14:57
1082	19:05	Taiyuang	9:32	N393	10:55	Xuzhou	21:03

(The above timetable <Nov. 2006 – June 2008> is just for your reference as it is subject to seasonal variations in spring and autumn. Please confirm the timetable with the Railway Station before you book the tickets.)

Rail Ticket Office:
Address: 2 Tai'an Road:
Tel: 82962777 / 82975022 Inquiry desk: 86011111
Telephones in use during renovation (Nov. 2006 - June, 2008)
Ticket booking: 95105105 Inquiry: 95105175
Railway ticket offices are available in a number of hotels.

Land Transportation

Qingdao is also a hub of a number of national highways such as Qingdao-Yinchuan (Northwest China), Tongjiang (Northeast China) - Sanya (South China), Jinan (Capital of Shandong Province) - Qingdao, Yantai (Northeast Shandong Province) - Qingdao, and Jiaozhou Bay Highway. The total highway distance in Qingdao alone reaches 524km, taking the lead in the cities in China. All the five satellite cities are within one-hour drive circle. Long-distance buses are offered in a dozen stations throughout Qingdao, with more than 400 routes to destinations in and out of Shandong Province.

Cities like Yantai, Weihai and Penglai in the northern Shandong Peninsula are easy of access, with a 3-4 hours bus ride.

The 4.5-hour express bus to Jinan is offered at the Long-distance Bus Station at 2 Wenzhou Road.

Long-distance Bus Stations

Name	Address	Telephone
Qingdao Municipal Station	2 Wenzhou Road	83718060
Guantao Road Station	49 Guantao Road	82825598
Qingdao Municipal Station (North)	59 Chongqing North Road	84820310
Qingdao Municipal Station (East)	33 Lishan East Road	88910011
Neimenggu Road Station	1 Hangzhou Zhi Road	82837924
Station at the Railway Station	Railway Station Square	82676842
Qingdao Part-load Transport Station	30 Lijin Road	83827731
Qingdao Second Station	40 Siliu North Road	84633252
Chengyang Station	Chengyang District	87869932
Huangdao Station	2 Changjiang West Road, Huangdao District	86973828
Jimo Station	30 Datong Road, Jimo City	88514289
Laixi Station	51 Qingdao Road, Laixi City	88467288
Pingdu Station	667 Shancheng Road, Pingdu City	88372008
Jiaozhou Station	11 Quanzhou North Road, Jiaozhou City	82262582
Jiaonan Station	1 Zhushan North Road, Jiaonan City	88194110

Normally, buses for destinations in and out of Shandong Province depart in the morning, while buses to the suburban cities are available every 20 or 30 mins.

The 84km Jiaozhou Bay Highway around the Bay connects Qingdao and Huangdao, one of its five districts, across the Bay in addition to the ferry service. The transport between the two places will be more facilitated when the transoceanic bridge is completed in 2009.

Public Bus Service Downtown

The hilly landscape of Qingdao makes it a paradise of public buses depriving the locals of bikes and motorcycles as popularly seen in other Chinese cities. Nowhere in Qingdao is inaccessible in the bus network maintained by the spacious buses in mint condition.

187 routes are in operation, and 3,752 buses, including trolley buses, run on the roads. Most of the buses are ticket-seller free and accept IC cards.

The fare is generally one yuan. Two yuan is charged for the airconditioned buses and a few luxury buses such as No. 501 and No. 801.

Starting from the Railway Station or the Ferry, buses No. 26, 202, 223, 304, 316, 321, 501 and No. 801 cruise along the seashore, with a number of scenic spots in view.

Bus No. 304, 311 from the Ferry and the Railway Station goes along the seashore to Laoshan Mountain.

Inquiry Desk for Public Bus Stations: 82817777

Taxi Service

Jetta and Santana are the majority of the taxies in Qingdao. It is not uncommon for taxies to detour a lot before reaching the destinations because single-way traffic is specially designed for the roads in Qingdao for the purpose of speeding up and easing the traffic jams. Disputes could be prevented between passengers and the drivers on which way to take if something is learnt beforehand about the local landscape.

Luxury type taxis charges a minimum of 10 yuan within 3 kilometers and 1.7 yuan/km beyond. The conventional type charges a minimum of 7 yuan within 3 kilometers and 1.2 yuan/km beyond.

An extra 0.4 yuan/km is charged for the rides from 22:00 in the evening to 05:00 of the next day.

It is advisable to ask for a receipt, for service supervision and any complaint.

Taxi Supervision/ Complaint Office: 83807661

Lost & Found Office: 83807502

Postal and Telecommunications Service

Over 500 post offices cover the 50,000km postal route, including EMS to 200 nations and regions.

IC card telephones are easy of access in all the public places, where various telephone cards are on sale.

Hundreds of Internet bars downtown facilitate going online for net-surfing.

Food and Beverage

The food industry in Qingdao is time-honored as shown by the household names of Tsingtao Beer, peanut oil and crab stick, to name just a few. The mineral water of Laoshan Mountain is a high-quality raw material used for brewing and for such beverages as coke, carbonated drinks, and table-water.

The Catering industry features sea food such as sea cucumber, scallop, abalone, whelk, prawn and porgy, as well as the farm produce of dried vegetables and mushrooms growing in the Laoshan Mountain. Heavy and salty flavor is typical of Shandong Cuisine, accompanied by other gourmet styles like Cantonese, Sichuan, Shanghai and northeast China. Spring and summer are the best seasons to enjoy the seafood especially when it goes with Tsingtao Beer and Laoshan Mineral Water.

It is not considered a real tour to Qingdao unless you have tried the seafood here. It is advisable to have the fresh seafood with garlic, vinegar and ginger for better taste.

When you are fed up with the delicacies and courtesies of hotels and restaurants, try to have a change in the food streets where you will be refreshed by the various flavors throughout the country.

Pichaiyuan Courtyard Food Street in Jiangning Road between Zhongshan Road and Hebei Road used to top the tourists' itinerary; but it has given way to the newly-emerging ones such as Zhongyuan

Food Street in Yunxiao Road, Xinzhan Food Street, Damaidao Seafood Street, Shuangxing (Double Star) Food Street, and Taishan Road Barbeque Food Street.

Top 10 Local Delicacies

- 小红楼灌汤包 (Xiaohonglou Guantangbao) Small steamed bun with stuff in soup inside from Xiao Honglou Restaurant
- 三鲜蒸饺 (Sanxian Zhengjiao) Steamed dumplings stuffed with shredded shrimp, pork and Chinese leek
- 天府元宵 (Tianfu Yuanxiao) Sweet dumplings from Tianfu Restaurant
- 长城三鲜水饺 (Changcheng Sanxian Shuijiao) Boiled dumpling stuffed with minced pork, shrimp and Chinese leek from Great Wall Restaurant
- 谷香村排骨面 (Guxiangcun Paigu Mian) Noodles with spare-ribs from Guxiangcun Restaurant
- 青岛大包 (Qingdao Dabao) Qingdao stuffed bun
- 青岛锅贴 (Qingdao Guotie) Qingdao pot stickers
- 大虾烧麦 (Daxia Shaomai) Steamed shrimp dumpling
- 海鲜馄饨 (Haixian Hundun) Seafood wonton
- 排骨砂锅米饭 (Paigu Shaguo Mifan) Pork ribs in clay pot and rice

Top 10 Seafood Snacks

- 瀛洲鲅鱼小吃 (Yingzhou Bayu Xiaochi) Spanish mackerel cooked in Yingzhou style
- 清蒸红岛海蛎子 (Qingzheng Hongdao Hailizi) Steamed Hongdao oyster
- 美格凉粉 (Meige Liangfen) Meige bean jelly
- 谷香村大虾面 (Guxiangcun Daxia Mian) Shrimp noodles from Guxiangcun Restaurant

- 瀛洲蛤蜊套餐 (Yingzhou Geli Taocan) Yingzhou set meal with clams
- 美达尔烤鱿鱼 (Meida'er Kao Youyu) Meida'er barbecued squid
- 大船光鱼套餐 (Dachuan Guangyu Taocan) Set meal with yarrella
- 砂锅全鱼 (Shaguo Quanyu) Whole fish in a clay pot
- 鲍鱼海鲜翡翠面(Baoyu Haixian Feicui Mian) Spinach noodles with abalone and other seafood
- 长城海鲜炉包 (Changcheng Haixian Lubao) Pan-fried buns stuffed with seafood from the Great Wall Restaurant

Local Restaurants

Name	Specialty	Address	Telephone
Shangri-la Hotel	Cantonese food,Shandong food	9 Xianggang Middle Road	83883838
Kylin Crown Hotel	Chinese food	197 Xianggang East Road	88891888
Sunshine & Holiday Hotel	Sea food, Shandong food	16 Xinzhan Road	83889888
Yinhai Restaurant	Sea food	30 Donghai Middle Road	85928222
Fengfeng Restaurant	Sea food, Shandong food	67 Xianggang West Road	83869777
Beidahuangren	Northeast flavor	3-7 Food Street, Damaidao Road	85930299
Beijing Deheng Roast Duck Restaurant	Roast duck	49 Nanjing Road	85782956
Xiaomingxuan	Sichuan flavor	161 Donghai Road	85782926
Brazil Barbeque	Barbeque	28 Minjiang 2nd Road	85731555
Jinghualou Beijing Roast Duck Restaurant	Roast duck	11 Fuzhou North Road	85768808
Hongwu (Red House) Steak	Steak	2F, Parkson, Zhongshan Road	82021176
Pizzahut	Pizza	63 Taidong 3rd Road	83672988
Lan Kwai Fong Restaurant, Nanjing Rd.	Cantonese food	11 Nanjing Road	85739688
Liangyoujindu Goumet Restaurant	Mongolian food, Northeast food	35 Donghai West Road	85815777
Mocuomen Tripe Restaurant at Shaoxing Rd.	Tripe hot pot	105 Shaoxing Road	85635089
Nanfang Restaurant	Special chicken in hot pot	46 Rehe Road	82829026
Nanfang Shark Fin Restaurant	Bird's nest, shark fin, abalone	69 Xianggang East Road	88011818
Yiqinglou Restaurant	Sea food, Shandong Food	1 Shantou Road	85967187
Yiqinglou Sea Food Restaurant	Sea food, Shandong Food	89 Ningxia Road	85825888

Name	Specialty	Address	Telephone
Yijing Lou	Seafood, Shandong Food	90 Xianggang Middle Road	85872018
Laochuanzhang Seafood World	Seafood	87 Changchun Road	83657999
Lilanfang Grandmother Restaurant	Seafood, Shanghai food	57 Guangxi Road	82961899
Zhongshanyuan Seafood Restaurant	Cantonese food, shark fins	33 Fuzhou South Road	85763333
Sanbao Congee Restaurant	Northeast food, congee	158 Minjiang Road	85722048
Qingdao Restaurant	Shandong food, sea cucumber	2 Shandong Road	83860098
Sitong Fish Pot Restaurant	Fish hot pot	20 Yunxiao Road	85784444
Taoji Rice Noodles	Yunnan rice noodles	45 Dacheng Road	83666178
Wangji Pickled Bone Restaurant	Pickled bone	149 Mingjiang 1st Road	85785222
Xiaoshaoxing Restaurant at Yunxiao Road	Boiled tender chicken — Shanghai Food	100 Yunxiao Road	85738088
Zhuxiangyuan	Boiled fish	116 West-2 Taidong 1st Road	83626970
Donglaishun Hot Pot	Shandong hot pot	26 Hangzhou Road	83731323
Fumanjia Congee Restaurant	Northeast seafood, congee	109 Minjiang Road	85772131
Guxiangcun Restaurant	Seafood—Shandong food	78 Henan Road	82821777
Qingdao Roast Duck Restaurant	Roast duck	174 Liaoning Road	83833559
Water Boiled Fish Restaurant	Sichuan food, hot pot	19 Yan'erdao Road	85920883
Hemingway Restaurant	Shandong food, Catonese food, family style dish	7 Shandong Road	85838958
Azhen Sea Cucumber Restaurant	Sea cucumber, seafood	30 Mingjiang 2nd Road	85730827
Chuanweiju	Sichuan food	58 Hunan Road	82965503
Gujierenjia	Sichuan, Shandong food	259 Ningxia Road	85718666
Laochuancai Restaurant	Sichuan food	107 Jiangxi Road	85759449
Chayuan Congee Restaurant	Shandong food, congee	174 Minjiang Roa	85715806
Longquan Mountain Villa	Mongolian food, Northeast food	Beizhai, Laoshan District	87059888

Name	Specialty	Address	Telephone
Yumatou Seafood Restaurant	Seafood, family style dish, Shandong food	28 Yunxiao Road	85735000
Dawanlai Restaurant	Sea food, family style dish, Shandong food	2 Shandong Road	83885667
Shunfeng Seafood Restaurant	Seafood	52 Xianggang West Road	83881818
Shuxiangyuan Restaurant	Sichuan food	118 Minjiang Road	85737122
Meida'er Grillroom	Shandong food, Barbeque	122 Minjiang Road	85713939
Tianfulaoma Restaurant	Sichuan, Shandong food	29 Jiangxi Road	85825360
Tianluyuan Sichuan Food Restaurant	Sichuan food	66 Taidong 3rd Road	83655857
Shunfeng Beef Restaurant	Beef hot pot	216 Yan'an 3rd Road	83896644
Xiaofeiyang Restaurant	Mutton hot pot	30 Donghai Middle Road	85921000
Yaoyao Hot Pot	Hot pot	17 Yanji Road	83621877
Daqinghua Dumpling Restaurant	Dumpling	56 Xianggang Middle Road	85753697
TV Tower Revolving Restaurant	Shandong food, Western food	1 Taipingshan Road	83639496
Qingdao Wanhechun Food Corporation	Special pork steak and rice	38 Taidong 8th Road	83663177
Haibianren	Roast, Shandong food	41 Minjiang 2nd Road	85711702

Other Snacks

- 冻菜凉粉 (Dongcai Liangfen) Agar-agar jelly
- 流亭猪蹄 (Liuting Zhuti) Liuting pig hoof
- 杠子头火烧 (Gangzitou Huoshao) Baked hard wheaten cake
- 锅饼 (Guobing) Paste pancake
- 合饼 (Hebing) Flapjack stuffed with egg and vegetables
- 甜沫 (Tianmo) Porridge made of millet and corn flour mixed with other vegetables
- 辣炒蛤蜊 (Lachao Geli) Fried spicy clams
- 烤鱿鱼 (Kao Youyu) Barbecued squid
- 地瓜枣 (Digua Zao) Dried sweet potato
- 大黄米元宵 (Dahuangmi Yuanxiao) Sweet dumplings made of gluti-

Name	Rank	Address	Telephone
Academic Exchange Center of Ocean University of China	★★★	5 Yushan Road	82931888
Eastern Light International Hotel	★★★	39 Shandong Road	85814688
Beihai Hotel	★★★	7 Xianggang Middle Road	83868888
Gongmao Hotel	★★★	17 Huayang Road	83836688
Qingdao Hotel	★★★	66 Xianggang Middle Road	85781888
Sanfod Hotel	★★★	96 Xianggang East Road	85897888
Qinchang Hotel	★★★	2 Huayan Road	83866988
Julinyuan Hotel	★★★	38 Biaoshan Road	83631888
Vienna Hotel	★★★	9 Aomen Road	83896688
Fuxin Mansion	★★★	5 Minjiang Road	85913688
Xindong Hotel	★★★	22 Fuzhou South Road	85777888
Xiushuiyuan Hotel	★★★	66 Tonghe Road, Pingdu City	87312208
Huayang Hotel	★★★	38 Heshan Road, Jimo City	87551666
Jiaozhou Dongfang Leyuan Hotel	★★★	Zhengfu Street, Jiaozhou City	88280800
Haidu Hotel	★★★	218 Changjiang Middle Road, Huangdao District	86999888

Shopping

Qingdao has long been known as an import and export center as well as a hub of manufacturing and banking. Consumer spending is constantly on the rise in this distribution center.

Shopping malls are easy to come by, including Liqun, Weekly, Gome, Sunshine Department Store, Le Printemps, Mykal, Jusco, Carrefour, Parkson, RT-mart and Wal-mart.

Zhongshan Road in the western part of Qingdao used to be the conventional shopping center before the eastern part was developed a decade ago. You can enjoy the night view of Zhongshan Road while strolling in such malls like Parkson, and the department stores like Guohuo and Dongfang. Printemps and Sunshine department stores are for high-end consumers, with Starbucks and Häagen-Dazs offered at Sunshine. Luxury items like LV, Prada, Gucci can be found in some exclusive shops in Crown Plaza Hotel of Xianggang Middle Road.

Bargaining might not work in Qingdao as the prices are already lower than in others areas of China and the local people tend to close the deal swiftly rather than talk around endlessly.

Formerly noted for its textile industry, Qingdao has now developed into a manufacturing center of household appliance, electronics, fashion, petrochemical and shipbuilding industries, apart from the previous light industry.

Local Specialties

Laoshan Stone Normally referred to as green stone or underwater jade, the stone can be carved into various handicrafts.

Xiantai Fish A freshwater fish tastes like cucumber, particular to the streams of Laoshan Mountain.

Laoshan Walking Stick With naturally-grown twists and turns, the camphor wood in Laoshan Mountain is used for making walking sticks.

Fist Fern Unique to Laoshan Mountain, the fern is dried before being fried or stewed with meat.

Bean Curd Made from Sheep Milk Made from sheep milk of Laoshan Mountain, the dairy product looks like bean curd.

Pine Mushroom Grown in the woodland of Laoshan Mountain, it is usually dried before being stewed with meat.

Straw-knitting Products Pingdu City boasts the best handicrafts made of straw such as hats, bags, baskets and mats, exported to over 50 countries and regions.

Shell Carving Handicrafts Originated in the 1960s, the shell carving handicrafts enjoy brisk sales at home and abroad.

Drawnwork As a traditional local handicraft, drawnwork is used for household decoration.

Poker Work It is a special painting by means of branding designs on sections of wood or plywood.

Budgerigar Also known as lovebirds, the birds with flamboyant colors are often raised in pairs.

Sorghum Candy The Candy remains the original fine and resilient taste with a history of 50 years.

Peanut and Its Products As a producing area of peanuts, Qingdao is well-acclaimed in the production of peanut oil, fried peanuts and peanut butter.

Man-made Crab Stick Made from imported fish flesh, it tasts like real crab.

Jiaozhou Chinese Cabbage The 400-year plantation history has contributed to the special flavor of the Cabbage.

Dazeshan Mountain Grapes Over 100 strains of grapes are grown in Dazeshan Mountain, nominated one of the 100 specialty hometowns in China.

Hawthorn Hawthorn produced in Laixi City is the best known; canned hawthorn likewise.

Calcium Enriched Milk Biscuit Good quality and rich nutrition makes the biscuit a preferred food for infants and children.

Sausage Famous processors include Wanxiangzhai, Dewei, Huaqing and Qinglian.

Kelp Shred Made of top quality kelp, it is a convenient food used at picnic.

Fish Fillet It is made from high quality ling.

Huadong Wine The famous brand names of wine include Italian Riesling, Chardonnay and Gamay.

Jimo Yellow Wine Based on its thousands of years' history, the Wine is one of the best yellow wines brewed in North China.

Laoshan Cola With Laoshan Mountain mineral water as the raw material, Laoshan Cola is one of the earliest of its kind in China.

Dried Shrimps The top-quality dried shrimp are produced in Shazikou Town.

Laoshan Tea Growing in the unique climate of Laoshan Mountain, Laoshan Tea has its own special taste.

Major Retailers

Sunshine Department Store

Address: 38 Xianggang Middle Road

Bus route: No. 12, 26, 31, 33, 104, 110, 125, 224, 225, 228, 231, 232, 304, 311, 312, 314, 316, 319, 321, 374, 501, 601, 701, 801, 802

Printemps Department Store

Address: 9 Shandong Road

Bus route: No. 32, 125, 202, 218, 220, 222, 224, 318, 322, 370, 374, 604, 605

Mykal Shopping Center

Address: 69 Xianggang Middle Road

Bus route: No. 31, 33, 104, 110, 125, 232, 304, 309, 311, 316, 321, 363, 501, 604, 801, 802

Parkson Department Store

Address: 44 Zhongshan Road

Bus route: No. 2, 5, 6, 8, 25, 26, 202, 217, 218, 220, 223, 225, 301, 304, 305, 307, 311, 312, 316, 320, 321, 501, 801, 802

Liqun Department Store

Address: 77 Taidong 3rd Road

Bus route: No. 1, 2, 3, 4, 11, 15, 30, 36, 104, 110, 119, 125, 205, 217, 218, 222, 226, 229, 232, 301, 302, 306, 307, 320, 367, 372

Liqun Sanbaihui Department Store

Address: 129 Yan'an Road

Bus route: No. 1, 4, 15, 25, 205, 212, 217, 219, 220, 225, 302, 306, 307, 308, 367, 368

Jusco Shopping Mall

Address: 72 Xianggang Middle Road

Bus route: No. 12, 31, 33, 104, 125, 208, 210, 224, 225, 228, 232, 304, 314, 316, 321, 363, 374, 501, 601, 801, 802

Guohuo (Domestic Goods) Department Store

Address: 149 Zhongshan Road

Bus route: No. 2, 5, 205, 218, 221, 222, 301, 305, 320, 366

Hualian Department Store

Address: 6 Feixian Road (next to Qingdao Railway Station)

Bus route: No. 2, 5, 8, 25, 26, 202, 217, 218, 220, 223, 301, 303, 304, 305, 307,

311, 312, 316, 320, 321, 501, 801, 802

Hualong Department Store

Address: 18 Jingkou Road

Bus route: No. 112, 113, 122, 128, 207, 213, 216, 230, 233, 361, 365, 378

Beifang Guomao Department Store

Address: 50 Xiangyang Road

Bus route: No. 9, 10, 102, 103, 105, 106, 109, 111, 112, 113, 114, 122, 123, 128, 129, 130, 207, 213, 230, 303, 306, 318, 361, 363, 365, 368, 371, 372, 605, 606

Carrefour (Mingda)

Address: 21 Xianggang Middle Road

Bus route: No. 12, 26, 31, 33, 104, 110, 125, 224, 225, 228, 231, 232, 304, 311, 312, 314, 316, 319, 321, 374, 501, 601, 701, 801, 802

Carrefour (Xinxing)

Address: 128 Shandong Road

Bus route: No. 3, 4, 28, 33, 119, 211, 224, 314, 318, 322, 365, 378

RT-mart

Address: 162 Ningxia Road

Bus route: No. 11, 202, 205, 220, 226, 227, 301, 309, 601

Meet All United Supermarket

Address: Intersection of Nanjing Road and Liaoyang Road

Bus route: No. 3, 4, 28, 36, 119, 126, 307, 308, 309, 362, 369, 370, 602

Qingdao Likelai Business & Trade Co., Ltd.

Address: 58 Jingkou Road, Licang District

Bus route: No. 112, 113, 122, 128, 207, 213, 216, 230, 233, 361, 365, 378

Zhongshan Underground Shopping Center

Address: 113 Zhongshan Road

Bus route: No. 2, 5, 205, 218, 221, 222, 301, 305, 320, 366

Longshan Underground Shopping Center

Address: 14 Longshan Road/ 29 Jiangsu Road

Bus route: No. 1, 214, 217, 220, 221, 225, 228, 231, 367

Taidong 3rd Road Pedestrian Mall

Address: Taidong 3rd Road

Bus route: No. 1, 2, 3, 4, 11, 15, 30, 36, 104, 110, 119, 125, 205, 217, 218, 222, 226, 229, 232, 301, 302, 306, 307, 320, 367, 372

Jimo Road Small Commodities Market

Address: Liaocheng Road

Bus route: No. 2, 5, 205, 212, 214, 218, 222, 301, 305, 308, 320, 366

Korean Fashion City

Address: Shichang 3rd Road

Bus route: No. 2, 5, 205, 212, 214, 218, 222, 301, 305, 308, 320, 366

Qingdao Hengdeli Clock, Watch, Glasses & Jewelry Co., Ltd.

Address: 170 Zhongshan Road

Bus route: No. 2, 5, 205, 218, 221, 222, 301, 305, 320, 366

Qingdao International Beer City

Address: Intersection of Xianggang East Road and Haier Lu

Bus route: No. 102, 104, 230, 301, 304, 362, 501, 802

Taishan Road Barbecue Street

Address: Taishan Road

Bus route: No. 8, 20, 24, 205, 217, 303

Yunxiao Road Food Street

Address: Section between Yunxiao Road and Minjiang Road

Bus route: No. 12, 26, 31, 33, 104, 110, 125, 224, 225, 228, 231, 232, 304, 311, 312, 314, 316, 319, 321, 374, 501, 601, 701, 801, 802

Beer Street

Address: Dengzhou Road

Bus route: No. 3, 205, 221, 302, 367, 368, 604

IT City

Address: 226 Liaoning Road

Bus route: No. 2, 5, 21, 24, 209, 211, 218,

221, 222, 301, 305, 320, 366

Qingdao Gome Electrical Appliance Store

Address: 80 Nanjing Road

Bus route: No. 12, 26, 32, 33, 125, 202, 210, 218, 220, 222, 312, 319, 322, 370, 601, 604, 701

Address: 48 Anshan 2nd Road

Bus route: No. 3, 4, 20, 28, 36, 119, 126, 209, 210, 211, 212, 219, 221, 229, 303, 306, 309, 310, 314, 319, 322, 362, 365, 368, 369, 372, 378, 602

Qingdao Suning Electrical Appliance Store

Address: 3 Nanjing Road

Bus route: No. 12, 26, 31, 33, 104, 110, 125, 224, 225, 228, 231, 232, 304, 311, 312, 314, 316, 319, 321, 374, 501, 601, 701, 801, 802

Haibo Furniture Store

Address: Zhenjiang North Road

Bus route: No. 3, 4, 28, 36, 212, 219, 306, 310, 314, 319, 322, 362, 368, 369

Qingdao B&Q Decoration & Building Materials Center

Address: 38 Shandong Road

Bus route: No. 2, 11, 33, 223, 224, 226, 227, 301, 308, 319, 322

Yan'an 2nd Road Wedding Dress Street

Address: Yan'an 2nd Road

Bus route: No. 1, 4, 15, 25, 205, 212, 217, 219, 220, 225, 302, 306, 307, 308, 367, 368

Book City

Address: 67 Xianggang Middle Road

Bus route: No. 12, 31, 33, 104, 125, 208, 210, 222, 224, 225, 228, 232, 304, 309, 314, 316, 321, 363, 369, 374, 501, 601,801, 802

Qingdao Cultural Market

Address: 3 Changle Road / 2 Yixian Road / 65-A Liaoning Road

Bus route: No. 2, 8, 211, 215, 217, 218, 221, 222, 232, 301, 320, 371

Bars and Teahouses

Name	Address	Telephone
Babyface Club	71 Xianggang Middle Road	85969898
Feeling Club	83 Xianggang Middle Road	85932929
Hongmen (Red Door) Bar	86 Shanghang Road	85932196
Xuan Bar, Shangri-La Hotel	9 Xianggang Middle Road	83883838-6402
Europe Bar, Kilin Crown Hotel	197 Xianggang East Road	88891888-6801
Honolulu Bar, Huiquan Dynasty Hotel	9 Nanhai Road	82999888-3277
Starbucks Coffee	38 Xianggang Middle Road	86677008
Jiandanrizi (Simple Days)	B 3-4, Fuhua Garden, 17 Yan'erdao Road	85886440
Corner Jazz Club	153-B Minjiang Road	85758560
Langyuan Bar	9-B Taipingjiao 2nd Road	83875734
Lennon Bar	20 Zhuhai Road	85893899
New York Club	2F, Huaqiao Hotel, Xianggang Middle Road	85739199
Shengdao Bar	55 Zhangzhou 2nd Road	85921398
Xiyinli (Charm) Bar	17 Yan'erdao Road	85923067
Alexander Coffee	36 Daming Road	83811663
SPR Coffee	Surf Plaza, 316 Xianggang East Road	88890400
Luoqi (Rocky) Bar	1 Building, Yongle Garden, 19 Yan'erdao Road	85927820
Meiri (Happy Day) Coffee	65 Xianggang Middle Road	85971179
Bi'an Coffee Bar	2 Jiangsu Road	82870377
Drip Drop Coffee	50 Zhangzhou 1st Road	85759937
Shangpin Coffee	149 Minjiang Road	85785626
Mingdian Coffee	22 Minjiang 2nd Road	85727233
UBC Coffee (Hengtai)	127 Liaoning Road	83812709
Xindian Coffee	20 Shantou Road	85727233
Lianhuage (Lotus) Teahouse	38 Minjiang 2nd Road	85782025
Mingquan Teahouse	14 Yunxiao Road	85760248
Mingcha Qiuhao Teahouse	201 Minjiang Road	85973767
Shiwai Taoyuan Teahouse	116-B Jiangxi Road	85783868
Zijinlian Teahouse	98 Jiangxi Road	85785125
Hongnihu Teahouse	15 Minjiang 2nd Road	85766019
Hexing Teahouse	52 Minjiang 2nd Road	85752781
QingyingeTeahouse	63 Xianggang Middle Road	85781598
Heyaxuan Teahouse	16 Xizhong 1st Road	83647557

Culture and Recreation

Being awarded one of the ten "Culturally Advanced Cities in China", Qingdao, otherwise known as Qindao meaning "Musical Instrument Island", has developed its own refined culture as represented by such international events as China International Violin Competition.

China International Violin Competition (CIVC) is convened in Qingdao every three years since the first one in 2005 at the People's Hall and the Music Hall of Qingdao University. Another venue for the Competition is the Music Hall at Lanshan Road. The contestants are from all over the world and the top winner in 2005 from Russia was awarded 20,000 US dollars. "Passionate Violin" is the logo and Mr. Lu Siqing, the renowned Chinese violinist, is the Publicity Ambassador for the Competition.

Radio, Broadcast and TV

China International Radio broadcasts to the globe in 39 languages and four Chinese dialects every day.

Local news in foreign languages is offered on QDTV-1 with Korean program at 6:00pm each Sunday and English program at 6:11pm each Sunday.

Press and Publication

Qingdao has two publishing houses — Qingdao Press and Press of Ocean University of China. A number of newspapers are issued such as *Qingdao Financial Daily*, *Qingdao Daily*, *Qingdao Morning*, *Qingdao Everning*, *Senior Citizen's Life* and *Peninsula Metropolis*, as well as such periodicals as *Merchants Weekly*, *Red Bubs*, *Little Sunflowers*, *China Juvenile Computer*, *Readers' Reference*, *Qingdao Pictorial*, and *Qingdao Literature*.

Culture and Entertainment

Qingdao Grand Theater, to be completed by 2008, tops all the cultural facilities of the City with the total investment of 650 million yuan. Covering 6 hectares with the floor area of 76,000m², it is located in the

east of Qingdao by the Shilaoren Beach and Qingdao International Beer City. The design, contributed by Germany's GMP Design Agency, is typical of the features of Qingdao — mountain, sea and city.

Qingdao Museum, located in the east of the city by the Beer City, covers the floor area of 20,000m^2 where antiques and artifacts unearthed in the peripheral areas of Qingdao are housed for display.

Qingdao Art Gallery in Daxue Road was opened in June, 2006. It is a traditional Chinese-styled building that used to be the site of Red Swastika and Qingdao Municipal Museum. Exhibitions are held on regular basis about the paintings of artists home and abroad.

Qingdao boasts fourteen troupes including the Peking Opera Troupe and Modern Drama Troupe. As a photography location for film and TV, Qingdao is home to a number of celebrities in entertainment circles, known as "Qingdao Phenomenon".

Integration of domestic and foreign culture is typical of Qingdao City as shown from the European-styled architecture in the western downtown area and the coffee houses and bars that spread over the city.

Various recreation activities with ocean characteristics, such as swimming and recreation on the sea are promoted by the government to enrich tourists' cultural activities.

Along with some local traditional festivals like Sugar-coated Hawthorn Festival, Radish Festival, Yangge (a folk dance) Festival in addition to the typical Spring Festival and Mid-Autumn Festival, the International Beer Festival, China Electronics Show, and Marine Festival add to the charm of the city.

The number of musical instruments, such as pianos and violins, leads the other cities across the nation. A tradition of teenagers' learning and playing musical instruments has crowned Qingdao as "An Island of Music".

The sea bestows some unique recreational opportunities upon Qingdao, such as swimming, yachting, powered-parachuting, sailing, beach volleyball and sand sculpture. *Gouji* — a local poker game involving six players – has seen its popularity beyond Qingdao and even beyond Shandong Province since the 1970s.

Local citizens' voluntarily feeding Seagulls in Qingdao Bay in the winter shows the harmonious coexistence between human and nature.

Tall, good-looking and well-built, the local people are talented in sports particularly football and athletics. Formerly known as the Football City and Track-and-field City, Qingdao is also a Sailing City boasting the national training center for water sports. With the sailing event of the 29th Olympic Games to be held in Qingdao, enormous effort has been made in developing the city into the national training center of waterborne sport.

Major Cinemas and Theaters

Name	Address	Telephone
Huiquan Cineplex	15-17 Nanhai 1st Road	82867219
Huachen Cineplex	69 Xianggang Middle Road	66700700
Wanda Cineplex	63 Taidong 3rd Road	83625656
China Cinema	97 Zhongshan Road	82865665
Daguangming Cinema	53 Taidong 1st Road	83633253
Taidong Cinema	28 Yunmen 1st Road	83801437
Yinhai Cinema	8 Anhui Road	82879924
Beijing Opera Troupe of Qingdao	76 Yan'an 1st Road	82739774
Qingdao Theater	12 Linqing Road	82818181

Museums and Memorials

Name	Address	Telephone
Qingdao Municipal Museum	27 Meiling Road	88897227
Qingdao Folk-custom Museum	19 Taiping Road	82880728
Qingdao Marine Products Museum	2 Laiyang Road	82868088
China Navy Museum	8 Laiyang Road	82866784
Qingdao Fire-control Museum	16 Jinhu Road	85816119
Qingdao Publication Art Gallery	77 Xuzhou Road	85830257
Qingdao Nanyuan Confucius Memorial	1 Qingdao Road	82892132

Bookstores and Libraries

Name	Address	Telephone
Shibei District Library	11 Daokou Road	83834425
Sifang District Library	67 Anshan 2nd Road	85632862
Laoshan District Library	19 Yunling Road	88894904
Qingdao Municipal Library	99 Shandong Road	85821021
Qingdao Archives	148 Yanji Road	85817777
Book City, Qingdao Xinhua Bookstore	67 Xianggang Middle Road	85875440
Xinhua Bookstore, Shinan Branch	10 Henan Road	82869414
Xinhua Bookstore, Shibei Branch	58-A Taidong 3rd Road	83655817
Xinhua Bookstore, Cangkou Branch	171 Zhenhua Road	84633233

Self-help Notes for Travelers

Public Security

It is inadvisable to carry a large amount of cash or valuable belongings especially in crowded areas even though good public order is acclaimed in Qingdao. Free of charge, the police telephone number of 110 also covers the service of 119 (fire alarm) and the service of 122 (traffic accident).

Visa

Foreign tourists are expected to apply for an entry visa at the local Chinese Embassy or Consulate.

The procedures for a group tour will be handled by the local travel agencies.

Taiwan compatriots may apply for the Chinese Mainland Travel Permit for Taiwan Residents at the China Travel Agency (Hong Kong) and the Office of the Commissioner of the Ministry of Foreign Affairs of PRC in the Hong Kong SAR.

Hong Kong and Macao compatriots may visit Chinese mainland with the Chinese Mainland Travel Permits for Hong Kong and Macao Residents.

Overseas Chinese may tour the mainland with valid passports issued by the competent authorities of the People's Republic of China, instead of applying for visas.

Customs

Inbound passengers are permitted to bring in, respectively, one piece of such items as camera, portable camera, mini video camera, portable video camera and portable word processor – for personal use. Extra articles shall be declared at the Customs.

Inward precious metals such as gold and silver (including their derivatives products) shall be declared if they exceed 50 grams. Gold and silver purchased in China shall be processed with a Special Invoice issued by the People's Bank of China.

Inward passengers are free to bring in an unlimited amount of foreign currency, traveler's checks and credit cards. The maximum amount of RMB brought in and out of China shall not exceed 20,000 yuan per person each time.

Identification issued by Chinese cultural administrations shall be produced, and detailed declaration shall be made to the Customs before carrying antiques out of China.

Chinese herbs for personal use, purchased with foreign currency, shall be processed in accordance with the current Customs regulations.

Business Hours and Public Holidays

Business hours of government departments, as well as some banks, are 8:30am – 5:30pm (including a one-hour lunch break), Monday through Friday.

Public holidays include New Year's Day (January 1), Spring Festival (January 1-7, Lunar Calendar), May Day (May 1-7), and National Day (October 1-7).

Currency

Only RMB issued by the People's Bank of China is acceptable in Qingdao.

The standard unit of RMB is yuan, with jiao and fen as subsidiary units. One yuan equals ten jiao, and one jiao equals ten fen. Yuan, jiao and fen are issued in both notes and coins.

RMB features the following 13 denominations: one hundred, fifty, twenty, ten, five and one yuan; five, two and one jiao; five, two, and one fen.

Coins are issued in six denominations: one yuan; five jiao and one jiao; five, two and one fen.

Foreign exchange service is offered at airports, hotels and souvenir stores in addition to the People's Bank of China.

Traveler's Checks and Credit Cards

Both traveler's checks and credit cards are acceptable in Qingdao. Traveler's checks can be cashed at the Bank of China.

Credit cards are acceptable in certain hotels, restaurants and stores.